PROPHETIC TREASURE

Revealing Hidden Secrets to the Holy Spirit's Transforming Presence

ROBERT STONE

Prophetic Treasure: Revealing Hidden Secrets to the Holy Spirit's Transforming Presence

Trilogy Christian Publishers
A Wholly Owned Subsidiary of Trinity Broadcasting Network
2442 Michelle Drive, Tustin, CA 92780

For information about special discounts for bulk purchases, please contact Trilogy Christian Publishing.

Trilogy Disclaimer: The views and content expressed in this book are those of the author and may not necessarily reflect the views and doctrine of Trilogy Christian Publishing or the Trinity Broadcasting Network.

10 9 8 7 6 5 4 3 2 1
Library of Congress Cataloging-in-Publication Data is available.

ISBN: 979-8-89041-037-5
E-ISBN: 979-8-89041-038-2

DEDICATION

I dedicate this book to the God and Father
of my Lord and Savior, Jesus Christ.
He has blessed me with all spiritual blessings in Christ
and continues to bless me each and every day.

To the Lord Jesus Christ,
who gave His life as a ransom for mine,
and to the Holy Spirit for His glorious
presence, understanding, and wisdom.

ACKNOWLEDGMENTS

I would like to acknowledge the following people who inspired me and encouraged me with their investment in the publishing of this book:

- My wife, Susan Stone.
- My children, Talitha, Tanyka, and Tyler.
- Dr. Kelley Varner.
- Dwight and Cynthia Karm.
- Tony and Becky Gariffo.
- Dr. Alfred Crane and Crowley Assembly of God.
- My brothers, David and Dennis Stone.
- Gerald and Linda Henegar.
- Pastor Lon McVeigh and Living Truth Church.
- Bishop Kevin and Pastor Sonjia Dickerson.
- Lyle and Maxine Horn.
- Pastor Michael Valiton.
- Elder Elnora Overton.
- Bernie and Neoma Cooksey.

TABLE OF CONTENTS

INTRODUCTION

We live in times of great uncertainty. Yes, similar seasons of time have happened before. But it is the rippling effects of the global economy, the concern over the possibility of a pandemic worse than the last one, and the lack of worldwide political leadership that has people feeling extremely anxious about the future. Along with this felt insecurity has come a lack of spiritual fervor. It has now been many, many years since God's people experienced a spiritual awakening that is anywhere near to the Protestant Reformation, the Great Awakening, or the Pentecostal and Charismatic movements.

They devoted themselves to the apostles' teaching and to the fellowship, to the breaking of bread and to prayer. Everyone was filled with awe at the many wonders and signs performed by the apostles. All the believers were together and had everything in common. They sold property and possessions to give to anyone who had need. Every day they continued to meet together in the temple courts. They broke bread in their homes and ate together with glad and sincere hearts, praising God and enjoying the favor of all the people. And the Lord added to their number daily those who were being saved.

— Acts 2:42–47 (NIV)

This spiritual and revolutionary change recorded by the gospel writer, Luke, is best explained in the Greek word *meta-tithemi*. *Metathithemi* means *to transpose, as when one thing is put in the place of another*.[1] Such transposition occurred through the death and resurrection of the Lord Jesus Christ, the outpouring of the Holy Spirit on the Day of Pentecost, and the supernatural ministry that flowed from the apostles and prophets of the first century.

This was the foundation of the gigantic ministry shift that took place in the first and second centuries. Luke wrote from his firsthand viewpoint in the book of Acts. Through Jesus' sacrificial death and resurrection, the priesthood of believers changed from the order of Levi to the order of Melchizedek (Hebrews 7:12). Along with this monumental change came the manifestation of the kingdom of heaven into and through the lives of men.

In the book of Acts, the manifestation of God's great grace by the Holy Spirit began assembling all of God's people (both Jew and Gentile) under the rule and care of the resurrected Lord Jesus Christ. Initially, those being saved experienced complete unity and solidarity with their Lord and each other. God was present in their hearts and minds, displaying His glorious Presence everywhere they met and went. Such caused the people to be in a complete relationship with Him (as beholding Him, face to face) and becoming intimately aware of the spiritual and prophetic treasures available to them.

Since the time of that first-century church, there have been many revivals, awakenings, and reformations. The Bible calls these "times of refreshing" (see Acts 3:19). Each of these spiritual seasons of blessing began as those in the known world were in spiritual crisis, anguish, or despair. Every season of refreshing or spiritual awakening has brought about the transformation from the old existence (think of a worn-out piece of clothing) to the establishment of a new, fresh, and dynamic spiritual reality (think of a new, beautiful, and expensive garment). Most began within a new group or family of people who became extremely hungry or thirsty for a new spiritual experience. They desired to embrace and experience the treasures of heaven. The majority sought to see their newfound reality fully and completely born into every tribe, race, and nation and to see the glory of God cover the earth as the waters cover the sea (Isaiah 11:9).

Scripture, as well as history, records a number of these spiritual transpositions. Each one has been an entrance into a new dimension of God's unfolding revelation (His proceeding word, see Matthew 4:4), His present truth (2 Peter 1:12), and a new or renewed revelation by the Holy Spirit, which proceeds from the Father (John 15:26). And now, I and others are seeing a coming prophetic shift on the spiritual horizon. There are places and people who are beginning to see the first signs of fresh spiritual understanding, accompanied by great signs and wonders. I have no doubt a new spiritual understanding will soon burst into our earthly dimension in a way that will be hard for many to perceive, understand, or even embrace.

Those who choose to embrace the coming prophetic reality will find entrance into a new spiritual dimension that will launch the church toward an even greater reality only realized in the glorious treasures found in Christ.

This coming new reality will be a season of glorious refreshing proceeding out of the Presence of the Lord (Acts 3:19). We, as God's holy people, have been called out of darkness into His light (1 Peter 2:9) so that we might experience the unfolding kingdom of heaven in its fullness. And this wonderful fullness will move us from glory to glory, faith to faith, and strength to strength in the coming days.

Come with me and embrace the coming restoration and crystallization of the prophetic ministry that is about to open greater and greater dimensions of heaven's treasure!

SECTION ONE:

Becoming Open to New Spiritual Realities

Each person's ability to experience heaven's prophetic treasures will ultimately be determined by their willingness to shift their mentality into one where spiritual growth and personal change are seen as a normal way of life. I can promise you that the results of fully embracing a life of growth and change will be so fulfilling that a person will never want to give up the rewards of this way of life (Hebrews 11:6). But I want to declare that the development of new spiritual and mental attitudes will require alert monitoring to ensure their continuity. Old beliefs, attitudes, and habits will do their best to reassert themselves if we are not vigilant. One must choose to develop a plan for dealing with them before the old way of thinking arises.

The first step toward that plan is found in one's willingness to embrace new spiritual adventures. Paul J. Meier said,

> *Many people live their lives in the shadow of public opinion, drifting with the tide of criticism, and wind-up wallowing in the backwash of mediocrity.*

Remember, no one can determine your desires, needs, or wants because no one else knows your priority of values or understands your potential. Be determined to have firm resolve, quiet confidence, and unshakable persistence. You will never go any higher than you are right now unless you dare to be numbered among the few who march to the beat of different drums—the drums that beat within you!

This new spiritual reality and subsequent transformation will give one entrance into new and exciting spiritual dimensions. Each life touched by God will also learn that genuine biblical understanding and spiritual wisdom flow from a life open to God and full of the Holy Spirit. The only true way is God's way. The only meaningful motivation is motivation based on the attitude and positive expectancy flowing out of the conviction that God has given us a bright hope and a future filled with His wonder and splendor (Jeremiah 29:11).

CHAPTER ONE:

New Adventures in the Prophetic

Learning to encounter, embrace, and enjoy the coming prophetic experience will not be founded in the things we do but rather in who we are willing to become. For if we are unwilling to become the person God will need us to be in the future, we will be regulated to living the life we are living now, which in the future, will become our *past life*. Instead of living in a new and exciting dimension of the Spirit, one will yearn for the days of yesteryear, a time when we found ourselves spiritually comfortable with who we were, the songs we sang, and satisfied with the accomplishments that eventually will continue to fade with time.

This describes many older Christians today who tragically embraced an escapism mentality.

This mentality was focused on "being ready to be raptured away." In the late nineteenth century and first two-thirds of the twentieth century, this approach to Christianity was the impetus for crusade evangelism. Missionaries and evangelists traveled the earth preaching to crowds of thousands and tens of thousands of people. Millions of people were saved for the purpose of preparing them for the "Lord's coming." But, at the same time, there was no focus on accomplishing societal transformation or personal spiritual maturity. *We now have tens of millions of Christians who have grown old in the Lord. But, instead of growing up in the Lord, most have focused on being ready to leave this world.*

Embracing the coming spiritual realities can only be fully accomplished as we open ourselves to all the wonderful possibilities the Spirit has to offer. Our becoming will continue to be a process, an intimate expression of who God wants us to be and become. Making the changes necessary for the spiritual growth of this type should probably be defined as *a personal reformation that will bring about a cultural revolution.* And honestly, for most people over the age of fifty, this will be very difficult. If we try to change our actions, habits, and ministries without monumental change happening first in our hearts, minds, attitudes, and beliefs, any change will be temporary.

It is our *being, becoming and being again,* that is the missing link in our development. As we grow, so shall we be. Becoming should not be seen as something that is of great cost "spent" by us, but rather seen as an investment being made in the future. It really doesn't matter about the price we may be required to provide; the investment will bring about huge dividends. What's relevant is what we get in return, which is our best life, the greatest life we could possibly live, as well as the change that will occur in the lives of our children, grandchildren, and subsequent generations. My friend, Dr. Kelley Varner, in his wonderful book *Secrets of the Ascended Life,* put it this way just before he went home to be with the Lord,

> *It is our being, becoming and being again, that is the missing link in our development.*

The application of the ascended life is the wisdom of Heaven for the situation of the earth. Every answer is in Him, and He has hidden Himself in you (Col. 1:27, 2:3). He has purposed to manifest, display, exhibit, and apply His wisdom in and through a many-membered, corporate Church.

One of the best ways to jeopardize our future in tomorrow's world and increase the probability of troubled times is to refuse to become today what we will need to be tomorrow. Who we will be and what we will be doing five years from now will be determined by the level of our commitment to Christ and our willingness to be shaped by His Presence. The amount of Scripture we learn, the books we read, the experiences we have, the concepts and precepts we embrace, the people we associate with, follow, and serve, as well as our willingness to embrace change and our openness to the Holy Spirit will ultimately determine what we will become.

Jesus came to His baptism after almost thirty years of obscurity and silence. The day He chose to leave His family and friends in Nazareth meant He had to leave those He loved the most behind. But at that moment, He chose to die to His adoptive father's way of life and fully embrace a new dimension of being in the person and purpose of His heavenly Father. This meant He had to embrace the life prophesied about Him by the prophet Isaiah.

The Spirit of the Sovereign LORD is on me, because the LORD has anointed me to proclaim good news to the poor. He has sent me to bind up the brokenhearted,

to proclaim freedom for the captives and release from
darkness for the prisoners, to proclaim the year of the
LORD's favor, and the day of vengeance of our God,
to comfort all who mourn, and provide for those who
grieve in Zion— to bestow on them a crown of beauty
instead of ashes, the oil of joy instead of mourning, and
a garment of praise instead of a spirit of despair. They
will be called oaks of righteousness, a planting of the
LORD for the display of his splendor.

— Isaiah 61:1–3 (NIV)

Like Jesus, the apostle Paul chose to embrace the spiritual
transformation God had planned for his life. In his address to
Governor Festus, Paul explained that he was the one whom the
Lord had prepared to be sent to Festus when he said,

But I have had God's help to this very day, and so I
stand here and testify to small and great alike. I am
saying nothing beyond what the prophets and Moses
said would happen—that the Christ would suffer and,
as the first to rise from the dead, would proclaim light
to his own people and to the Gentiles.

— Acts 26:22–23 (NIV)
(emphasis added by the author)

Sent first to their own people, the Jews, both Jesus and Paul
saw and treated people of Abrahamic decent as God's treasured
people (Exodus 19:5) and as sheep without a shepherd (Matthew
9:36). Yet, both knew that their ministry and service was meant

to extend to both the Jews and Gentiles. Paul wrote the church in Rome that we believers in Christ, who are not of Jewish decent, are like a wild olive shoot that has been grafted into the planted and domesticated olive tree (the Jews) and now share in the nourishing sap from the olive root (Christ Jesus, see Romans 11:17). The Holy Spirit's ministry is to both Jew and Gentile!

Believers of every race are God's treasured people and should respond as such! As His treasured people, let us first declare and minister to the Lord with King David,

> *Praise be to you, LORD, the God of our father Israel, from everlasting to everlasting. Yours, LORD, is the greatness and the power and the glory and the majesty and the splendor, for everything in heaven and earth is yours. Yours, LORD, is the kingdom; you are exalted as head over all. Wealth and honor come from you; you are the ruler of all things. In your hands are strength and power to exalt and give strength to all. Now, our God, we give you thanks, and praise your glorious name.*
>
> — 1 Chronicles 29:10–13 (NIV)

Even now, the Holy Spirit is seeking to manifest the Lord Jesus Christ and new spiritual realities in and through each of our lives. Our embrace of this manifestation will reveal Him, as well as the treasured values we see in the life of Jesus (as He walked here on Earth), which include those I will address in this book. When others see His Presence and wisdom being manifested in and through you, they will see Jesus. This means they will see Jesus when you pray, when you praise, and when you minister.

The Spirit desires to display new and wondrously glorious treasures in and through all the people of the earth. He seeks to bless the people of the earth through us with good things.

CHAPTER TWO:

Hunting for Treasure

Over the past several decades, there has been a definite decrease in the interest of spiritual things within the United States of America. But we are not alone. In other cultures and countries across the globe, the depletion of faith, virtue, self-control, godliness, and basic goodness has occurred despite the expansion of evangelism and the availability of biblical knowledge (both of which are a result of the internet and the plethora of biblical information and teachers). These values and many others that were once treasured by all peoples—not just Christians—have been assaulted on a scale not seen since the dark ages.

There has been almost a complete demise of the prophetic ministry in the last twenty years.

But even more than the erosion of biblical values, there has been almost a complete demise of the prophetic ministry in the last twenty years. Yet, this should be of no surprise. For Jesus gave several warnings that having faith in God and His Christ would bring about persecution and derision, as well as trouble (Matthew 5:11 and John 16:33). Paul warned the Thessalonians that they should "not treat prophecies with contempt" and that there would come a "great falling away" (1 Thessalonians 5:20; 2 Thessalonian 2:3, NIV) as the end of time came into view. Simply put, according to statistics, there has been and continues to be a lack of interest in spiritual things, even among Christians in many parts of the world.

Perhaps most disconcerting has been the depletion of the number of believers who believe and participate in spiritual gifts (especially prophecy) and the supernatural. During the 1980s and '90s, there was a dramatic rise in people interested in the Pentecostal, Charismatic, and Word of Faith movements. From books to satellite networks, along with a plethora of Christian television programs, church revivals, and seminars, millions of people sought to experience the supernatural and especially the dynamic spiritual gifts listed in 1 Corinthians 12 and 14.

During this time, there was a flurry of apostolic and prophetic ministry, including prophetic words, healings, and supernatural acts of deliverance. The events of the Y2-K debacle and the 9-11 attack in New York brought even greater interest, but it only lasted for a short season. That season soon faded, and over the last twenty years, the spiritual decline in America has caused many churches and ministries that once flourished to either close or adjust to focusing on providing "loaves and fishes" instead of leading people into the deep things of God.

In his *January 2020 State of the Church Report*, George Barna listed three things that offer proof for these remarks. The first and perhaps most significant change is that practicing Christians are now a much smaller segment of the entire United States of America population. Along with that, the report states the growth in number of those who see themselves as atheist or agnostic has doubled in size over the past twenty years. And lastly, thirty-six percent fewer Americans attend church each week than they did in 1993.[2] And all of this took place before the COVID-19 pandemic forced many churches to suspend their worship services or simply move to doing them online.

With these things in mind, I would like to ask a few questions. What kind of things do you consider valuable? Where would your list begin? What would it include? What are the spiritual values that you consider to be important? And why would you include them?

Does your list begin with spiritual, mental, or natural things? If you are not sure how to answer, I encourage you to start with the people and things that you appreciate, treasure, and consider of great worth. Perhaps you should begin with the small things you consider your "personal valuables." To enlarge your list, include a special item you inherited or purchased, like a painting, a piece of jewelry, or a coin. Maybe you would consider adding to your list the family pictures that have been handed down to you from your parents, grandparents, or previous ancestors. Then add the people you love or something intangible, like your love for the Lord, your spouse, or your friends.

And what about the things of God? Do you see the Word of God, the people you attend church with, your chosen style of praise and worship, or the demonstration of spiritual gifts as things to be treasured? Which of the spiritual values written about in the Bible do you think of as important? And why? Then consider the whole list and sort it out from most to least important to you. Then, let me ask, where are your spiritual values on the list?

During the seventeenth and eighteenth centuries, the number of pirates and pirate ships flourished in and around the western

Atlantic Ocean and the Caribbean Sea. During that time, it has been estimated that there were between four and five thousand pirate ships sailing the high seas. Over the last ninety years, Hollywood has made pirates and piracy famous with movies such as *Blackbeard, Treasure Island*, and the *Pirates of the Caribbean* series. Each movie has been filled with great adventure, excitement, and a host of characters. Most of the pirates have been depicted as swashbuckling, sword fighting, eye patch wearing, rum drinking, and audacious raiders. But practically every one of these movies has centered around one theme: t*he hunt for hidden or buried treasure.* In almost every story, the hunt to find the treasure begins with a *treasure map that has an X that marks the "spot"* where the treasure can be found. Most of Hollywood's renditions have been filled with great drama, dreams of striking it rich, a succession of hits and misses (of finding the treasure), as well as overcoming a host of problems and other people who seemed bent on finding and keeping the treasure for themselves.

Today, there aren't many pirates sailing around the Caribbean looking for treasure. But the hunt for treasure continues. In August of 2022, *Fox News* reported on a treasure trove that had been uncovered off the coast of the Bahamas. A seventeenth-century ship named Maravillas sunk off the Little Bahama Bank in the Northern Bahamas on January 4, 1656. It had been carrying numerous treasures of both royal tax and private property.[3]

The remains of the ship were scattered over the ocean floor, and for more than 360 years, archeologists and adventurers attempted to locate the ship's debris and treasure. Once located, almost half of the estimated 3.5 million pieces of treasure were salvaged between 1659 and the end of the twentieth century. But thanks to modern-day technology, the Allen Exploration team found new riches beyond imagination.

In seawater of only about fifty feet, the Allen team found cannons, anchors, emeralds, and amethysts, as well as about 3,000 silver coins and twenty-five gold coins. This fascinating find also included Spanish olive jars, Chinese porcelain, and iron rigging. The team also discovered a silver sword handle belonging to the soldier Don Martin de Aranda y Gusmán; the item helped the team identify these treasures as belonging to the sunken Maravillas. There have been several gorgeous pieces of jewelry found, including five beautiful pendants. One is a golden pendant with the Cross of Santiago designed in the shape of a scallop shell, and four more pendants worn by members of the sacred Order of Santiago. Artifacts from a religious band of knights active in Spanish maritime trade were also recovered.[4]

There has always been a certain allure about finding hidden treasure. When we see someone using a metal detector along the beach or in a park, it is because they are looking for some sort of lost treasure. The number of Americans buying lottery tickets or visiting casinos (in hopes of *winning it big*) grows with each passing year. The internet is filled with no end of advertisements that guarantee to direct individuals toward finding the next great treasure. Gigantic promises of great wealth are promised to be just a click away. A person just needs to find the right investment or opportunity, whether it will be found in bitcoin, precious metals, the stock market, and even real estate, to strike it rich.

What type of treasure are you looking for? What does your heart seek?

The people and things we humans consider valuable are precious, desirable, or cherished by us. Such things are dear to our hearts, our feelings, and our emotions. There are two foundational truths concerning the things we value. First, as a noun, the word value comes from the Latin word *valor* (from *valeo*). It means *to be of worth*. Noah Webster defined value as,

> *Property or those properties of a thing which render it useful or estimable. The* real value *of a thing is its utility, its power or capacity of procuring or producing good. Hence the* real or intrinsic value *of iron, is far greater than that of gold. But there is, in many things, an estimated* value *depending on opinion or fashion, such as the* value *of precious stones, that make them more precious than iron. The* value *of land depends on its fertility, or on its vicinity to a market, or on both.*[5]

Second, the word value can also be used as a verb. In Webster's 1828 Dictionary, its use as a verb is defined as,

> *To estimate the worth of something: as to* value *lands or goods. Or, to have in high esteem, as a* valued *poem or picture. In essence it means to esteem; to hold in and estimation; as, to* value *one for his works or virtues.*[6]

Let's address the perceived and real value of spiritual treasure, especially that of prophetic gifts and ministry. In prior generations, such were either held in the highest regard or disdained to the point that those recognized for their prophetic ministry were persecuted, jailed, and even murdered (Luke 11:47–48). And yet, the Holy Spirit of God is more than willing to reveal to each of us this wondrous treasure of heaven. He seeks to give directions to those who are traveling the narrow pathway of righteousness as well as the inspiration needed to lay up treasures in heaven. It is also true (as Moses told Joshua) that "I wish that all the LORD's people were prophets and that the LORD would put his Spirit on them!" (Numbers 11:29, NIV).

To begin our quest, let's look at *intrinsic value*. Such is generally determined by what a person or persons consider valuable. For the most part, the value of something is tied to the price one pays for it. Intrinsic value is the value that a thing has "in itself," or "for its own sake," or "as such," or "in its own right."[7] You may not have paid for the things you value, but it is likely that someone did. Such valuables are loved, prized, and revered. In the modern age, many consider time to be more valuable than money. And one's management of time is greatly affected by the value placed on it by the individual.

When it comes to the Scripture and the manifestation of spiritual gifts, that which is deemed most valuable is also called, in a spiritual sense, treasure. And like the hidden treasure found in the pirate movies, spiritual treasure speaks not only of something very valuable but, for the most part, it is concealed or hidden. That is where the prophetic ministry and the illuminating power of the Holy Spirit come in.

Prophetic people tend to be spiritual detectives or investigators. They are always in search of the hidden and deep things of God. The illumination, inspiration, and revelation their insight and ministry provide to the body of Christ are invaluable to all of us. For without such, God's people soon begin speculating about different theologies and philosophies, including offering

Prophetic people tend to be spiritual detectives or investigators.

opinions based on the writings of Sigmund Freud and Carl Jung instead of comparing Scripture with Scripture and embracing our society's desperate need for the manifestation and administration of spiritual gifts.

Early biblical writers used three Hebrew words when speaking about treasure. The first of these was used by Moses. He used the Hebrew word *matmon*, which literally means "a secret storehouse." The word was usually used to describe where money or hidden riches of any kind were buried. Moses said Joseph used this word to describe the silver he had hidden in his brother's sacks in Genesis 43:23 (NIV), "'It's all right,' he said. 'Don't be afraid. Your God, the God of your father, has given you *treasure* in your sacks; I received your silver'" (emphasis added by the author).[8]

Moses, inspired by the Holy Spirit, used his experience with Egyptian culture to describe heavenly things that are beyond the scope of the natural man. No doubt Moses understood the power of spiritual mystery and revelation. He had witnessed firsthand, as an Egyptian prince, some of the earliest treasure safes or vaults first built by the Egyptians.

Over the last hundred and twenty years, archeologists have made several exciting discoveries of hidden and protected vaults in several of the Egyptian pyramids. This tells us that early Egyptians saw the construction of hidden vaults as being important to them, especially in the keeping of certain items that were deemed valuable. In fact, several Egyptian kings built huge pyramids with larger and larger hidden burial chambers that they filled with huge amounts of personal treasures. These burial vaults were constructed to protect their "valuables" from robbers and thieves as well as from anyone who would interfere with the Pharoah's journey into the afterlife. Many precious and wonderful paintings, as well as beautiful sculptures made from gold and other precious metals, have been found in many of these hidden tombs. This tells us that for at least the last four to five thousand years, people have deemed certain things valuable enough to have them stored somewhere "safe."

The other two similar Hebrew words translated as value or treasure are *mikhman* and *saphan*. The first speaks not only of the hiding place but of the value of the item or items hidden there. In the prophet Daniel's description of the end of time, he speaks of the conflict between the political powers of Earth and heaven, which ultimately determine who gains control of the great treasures of gold and silver.

> *At the time of the end the king of the South will engage him in battle, and the king of the North will storm out against him with chariots and cavalry and a great fleet of ships. ...He will gain control of the treasures of gold and silver and all the riches of Egypt.*
>
> — Daniel 11:40, 43a (NIV)

Saphan speaks specifically to hidden treasures or valuables that are concealed.[9] In Moses' prophecy concerning Zebulun, he said,

> *Rejoice, Zebulun, in your going out, and you, Issachar, in your tents. They will summon peoples to the mountain and there offer sacrifices of righteousness; they will*

feast on the abundance of the seas, on the treasures hidden in the sand.

— Deuteronomy 33:18–19 (NIV)

These Hebrew words speak to one concept. That which is seen as having great value is usually hidden, stored away, and kept safe (Proverbs 15:6). Such descriptive language was also employed by Jesus many times. He taught that things that are considered great in value or treasured (it can be either material treasure, like money or other valuable material possessions, or spiritual treasure, i.e., our relationship with God) is usually hidden.

Speaking of spiritual treasure, Jesus taught the kingdom of heaven itself is like a treasure hidden in a field (Matthew 13:44) or like that of good treasure that is hidden away in the heart (Matthew 12:35). Other references Jesus used when speaking of hidden spiritual treasure can be found in Mark 10:21 and Luke 6:45; 12:33; 18:22.

Jesus also told His disciples when they asked why He spoke so often in parables, "The knowledge of the secrets [the Greek *musterion* for hidden things] of the kingdom of heaven has been given to you, but not to them" (Matthew 13:11, NIV).

All human beings have certain possessions they consider as valuable and precious. They are intrinsically valuable because of the price that was paid for them or because they became valuable due to their importance. And like the Egyptians and Romans, we seek to keep our valuables *safe*. The two words, *valuable* and *safe*, have become interconnected. That which we see as valuable, we try to keep safe. And that which we save is seen as valuable (at least to us).

When we value items of personal property, like our cell phone or our retirement account, we do our best to keep those things safely hidden from thieves or any destructive force that might steal or destroy them. Yet, in this modern age keeping our valuables safe is growing increasingly more difficult. I'm sure most of us would agree that keeping young children safe should be a priority in our society (because they are valuable). And yet, in the United States of America, we continue to suffer such incomprehensible catastrophes as abortion on demand (still available in many states) and the mass murders of children in elementary and secondary schools (such as what happened in Uvalde, Texas, in 2022). We have witnessed too many murders of innocent children as well as the lost lives of thousands of teenagers overdosing on cocaine, heroin, oxycodone, and now, fentanyl.

Many of the things that we hold dear are being assaulted as never before. Computer hackers are ever on the prowl to loot our personal or financial information. Insurance companies and financial institutions are finding it almost impossible to build secure enough firewalls to protect our private and personal information. Billions of dollars and millions of man-hours are being spent each year in trying to keep our families, Social Security numbers, financial accounts, and even private medical information secure.

Almost two thousand years ago, Jesus spoke about this matter of valuables being kept safe in Matthew 6:19–21 (NIV). He said,

> *Do not store up for yourselves treasures on earth, where*
> *moths and vermin destroy, and where thieves break*
> *in and steal. But store up for yourselves treasures in*
> *heaven, where moths and vermin do not destroy, and*

where thieves do not break in and steal. For where your treasure is, there your heart will be also.

Apparently, even in His day, those who lived in Israel found it difficult to keep their personal and spiritual valuables safe. Jesus also knew that the physical and tangible things of this life are always passing away either with time, deterioration, or theft, while the righteous and the eternal treasures found in Christ can be held in heaven's vault and kept safe forever.

The Lord's instruction in Matthew provides us prophetic insight into the things that should take priority and how things of great value are kept secure in heaven. In both His teaching and life, Jesus focused on eternal principles that established both spiritual and everlasting value. In other words, Jesus both taught and lived a life filled with and focused on the treasures of heaven. His preaching and teaching concentrated on revealing the eternal values of His heavenly Father. This is the work for which He was sent to do (to reveal that which is truly valuable and add spiritual value to others).

Therefore, He focused on revealing the values of the kingdom of heaven to mankind. Jesus wanted each person to both see and know that they were intrinsically valuable to God (who they are) and extrinsically valuable (what they could become in Christ). Jesus proved His commitment to such by laying down His eternally pre-existent heavenly life and embracing His earthly life for the purpose of purchasing and providing eternal salvation for all who are willing to believe and call on His Name.

His act of self-sacrifice is established in Scripture as the highest price that could ever be paid. With that price, He redeemed mankind from the penalty, power, and presence of sin. He paid a debt He did not owe. While we owed a debt we could not pay. And, because we humans are God's most valuable possession and because He paid the ultimate price for our redemption through His sacrifice on the cross, shouldn't we fully embrace the spiritual values that will not rust or be stolen away?

The kind of life I am proposing to you doesn't happen without passionate and intentional commitment. One does not drift or stumble into spiritual transformation of heart and soul. One must make a spiritual commitment and pray for a clear path to grow up and become mature in Jesus Christ. This type of spiritual intention requires us to involve our whole heart, soul, mind, and strength. This type of relationship with the Lord Jesus must not be viewed with a lukewarm or hapless commitment. Effort must be consistently exerted. And positive and continued progress will call for our total devotion, great fervor, and passionate zeal.

Today, I am praying that you will become more willing to enter a new level of relationship and fellowship with the Holy Spirit. I encourage you to embrace a new dimension of thanksgiving, praise, worship, prayer, and Bible study. I pray that even now, you will choose to be generous and seek to bless others rather than keeping the blessing for yourself—not because you are forced to do so or are manipulated into such, but rather because you love the Lord Jesus Christ and your greatest desire is to honor, submit to, and serve Him.

I also pray that as you enter through this new doorway, you begin walking into new and more glorious dimensions of the Holy Spirit, that your spiritual understanding and wisdom will be raised beyond the level where you currently are, and that you experience a higher dimension of the Spirit's illumination and revelation.

Through the words of this book, I believe the Lord is offering a new opportunity to you. An opportunity to fully explore, experience, embrace, and enjoy the treasures of heaven, as well as to participate in the coming unprecedented move of God, which may just be the last one prior to Christ's return. These treasures are first to be embraced and enjoyed and then shared with those God has placed in your life. God's greatest treasures cannot be devalued by inflation, stolen by thieves, or destroyed by the storms of life. In essence, *we must follow His example.*

CHAPTER THREE:

God's Treasure Chest

"In the beginning God created the heavens and the earth. ...And God said, 'Let there be light'"

— Genesis 1:1, 3 (NIV)

The Lord, the LORD Almighty— he touches the earth and it melts, and all who live in it mourn; the whole land rises like the Nile, then sinks like the river of Egypt; he builds his lofty palace in the heavens and sets its foundation on the earth; he calls for the waters of the sea and pours them out over the face of the land— the LORD is his name.

— Amos 9:5–6 (NIV)

To understand God's process of revealing His prophetic secrets (Amos 3:7), we must begin at the beginning. In the beginning, God created the heavens and the earth. His creation began with Him speaking His light into complete existence (spiritual, mental, emotional, and physical). One cannot speak intelligently of that which one does not know. In God's case, He not only knew about light and all the properties of light, but

He is light, and there is no darkness in Him (John 1:5). Light and the understanding of light play an important part in every spiritual outpouring, renewing and season of refreshing. I will address the revelation of spiritual light later in this book, but first, I want to help you understand the place God's light was first manifested. That place is called heaven.

Contrary to what many think, heaven is not merely a state of mind or being but a true and real place. Many modern men and women see heaven as some religious and idyllic fantasy held on to by illogical and irrational people. Even many modern Christians only see heaven as an eternal vacation resort shrouded by a sort of ethereal mist. Others believe it is a place where those who have crossed over to the other side have become angels and now float on white puffy clouds with little or nothing to do. Due to countless humans around the world having more material things than ever before, any real thought about the place called heaven and eternity has been relegated to the terminally ill, the very elderly, or some illogical group of Christians.

The Bible says that the eternal God is the creator, owner, and possessor of heaven. Moses said, "To the LORD your God belong the heavens, even the highest heavens [or the heaven of heavens], the earth and everything in it" (Deuteronomy 10:14, NIV). The psalmist David also spoke of heaven being more than just a place, but God's home. Psalm 11:4 (NIV) says, "The LORD is in his holy temple; the LORD is on his heavenly throne." In Ezekiel's heavenly vision, heaven (Hebrew word, *heykal*) is revealed as the magnificent palace of God, the great and eternal king. He included in his prophecy that heaven is more than just a place, but the temple, the home, and the dwelling place of the God of the ages (Ezekiel 8:16). Because God is light and there is no darkness in Him at all, *heaven is the first place filled with the glory of God's light.*

We human beings like to fill our homes with things we appreciate and love. So, it is with our Lord. The Scriptures leave no doubt that heaven is a place filled with God's great and marvelous treasures. Light, life, love, joy, and eternal peace are just a few of the magnificent riches hidden in God's original treasure house. There is coming a time when the saints of all the ages will gather in heaven's light to offer thanksgiving, praise, and worship to the Most High God and the Lamb for revealing heaven's treasures (beginning with light) and sharing them with us who have been born and have lived our lives on the earth. And according to Jesus Christ, the Son of God, heaven is also the place He came from and would return to. He said, "No one has ever gone into heaven except the one who came from heaven—the Son of Man" (John 3:13, NIV) and, "Jesus said to them, 'If God were your Father, you would love me, for I have come here from God. I have not come on my own; God sent me'" (John 8:42, NIV).

What else makes heaven so important? It was the first place created by the spoken Word of God. In the beginning, God created the heavens and the earth, and He did so by His own spoken word. In the book of Genesis, Moses used two different words in his writings to describe heaven. By using the Hebrew words *miqqedash* and *shamayim*, Moses describes heaven as the place where God and all His attributes dwell. Both nouns speak directly to the visible heavens (which includes the earth's atmosphere and the remainder of the physical universe) and the heaven of heavens. It is the heaven of heavens that the Bible describes as the residence, or sacred and holy sanctuary of the one true, living, and eternal God. And again, heaven is a righteous place full of God's light, life, and love. It is also filled with heaven's most valuable treasure, God Himself.[10]

There shall be no end to God's goodness and glory that floods and fills the atmosphere of heaven. This should encourage us to reach for the heavens and seek to fully experience the treasures of such a place! Heaven is a place where believers in Jesus Christ will go after their life on Earth ends. It is also the place we will return from with the Lord Jesus (1 Thessalonians 3:13). The most glorious attribute that we humans should see about heaven is found in the blessedness of God's Presence experienced there. From the moment we enter heaven, we will experience unfettered, constant, and harmonious holy personal union with the Lord God Almighty (Father, Son, and Holy Spirit) forever and ever.[11]

According to the book of Revelation, it is in that place believers will encounter the Lamb of God face to face in all of His glory (Revelation 4:11, 5:13)! The saints of God will be led by the Lamb to living fountains of water and the tree of life. Both of which will be found in the middle of the paradise called the New Jerusalem. In that place, the saints from every tribe, nation, and people will stand as one vast "temple." We will gather there, surrounding the Lord God Almighty and the Lamb, declaring our eternal allegiance and worship. We, who are His holy temple, shall be God's king-priests reigning and serving forever.[12]

> *You will bring them in and plant them on the mountain of your inheritance—the place, LORD, you made for your dwelling, the sanctuary, Lord, your hands established. "The LORD reigns for ever and ever."*
>
> — Exodus 15:17 (NIV)

I pray you see that heaven is more than streets of gold and walls of jasper. It is a real location where the righteous creatures and inhabitants of heaven are now and will forever live in the eternal blessedness of God's Presence, either in the new heaven or new earth. In heaven, there is no sin, no suffering, or death. His blessing is upon all who are there. His bless-ing includes the most magnificent love, peace, and joy that can ever be experienced. Heaven's inhabitants include not only the eternal God but created beings He created in both heaven and Earth. Heaven's beings and those saved by His grace now possess God's everlasting life and eternal weight of glory (2 Corinthians 4:17), an exemption from all future suf-fering as well as a complete and full deliverance from all evil (2 Corinthians 5:1–2). They shall, without termination, live in His "fulness of joy" forever.[13]

In heaven, there is no sin, no suffering, or death.

In the book of Deuteronomy 28:12 (WTT), Moses used a different Hebrew word for heaven (*owtsar*). He did so to speak of heaven as a hiding place, treasure house, storehouse, or vault where God's spiritual and natural supplies are hidden away and kept for safekeeping.

> *The LORD will open the heavens, the storehouse of his bounty, to send rain on your land in season and to bless all the work of your hands. You will lend to many nations but will borrow from none.*

As a storehouse, *the heaven of heavens or third heaven* (see 2 Corinthians 12:2) holds in store the glorious attributes and blessings of the Almighty and loving God. These attributes and blessings (the fullness of the Deity) are now found and revealed in Christ Jesus in bodily form (Colossians 2:9). Gaining understanding about who God is, is best understood through the insight or light provided us in the Word of God and by the prophetic ministry. It is the prophets of old that were the first to shine the light on the names used to reveal the one true, infinite God to whom we, created and finite human beings, worship. The apostle Peter said,

> *We also have the prophetic message as something completely reliable, and you will do well to pay attention to it, as to a light shining in a dark place, until the day dawns and the morning star rises in your hearts. Above all, you must understand that no prophecy of Scripture came about by the prophet's own interpretation of things. For prophecy never had its origin in the human will, but prophets, though human, spoke from God as they were carried along by the Holy Spirit.*

> — 2 Peter 1:19–21 (NIV)

Through prophetic utterances given by Abraham, Moses, and David, the names of God, like Elohim, Jehovah-Jireh, Jehovah-Shalom, and Jehovah Nissi, offer fresh revelation concerning the relationship of God to His people. By prophetic revelation, the Hebrew people declared God by these and other names. Each name was used to declare, describe, and disclose His divine person. He revealed Himself as Yahweh, Tsur, and Adonai, as well as more revelatory combination names, like El-Shaddai, Jehovah Rapha, and many others.[14]

I believe that the most distinguishing Name of God in the Old Testament is the Name transliterated into English as Jehovah-Jireh. It is Jehovah-Jireh that declares Yahweh as the Hebrew people's supplier of their every need. It also speaks to God as both *being* and *having* a "storehouse." That storehouse is called *heaven*. It is Abraham, who by use of the name Jehovah-Jireh, declares the God Abraham and his descendants serve as *being and having* the total supply to meet *each and all* of our needs. Because God's dwelling place is heaven, God Himself and His home (heaven) is His storehouse, depository, cellar, garner, and armory. But more than a place, it speaks to the hidden treasure or valuables stored there, including God Himself. The English Revised Version and the American Standard Revised Version both translate the word for heaven (*owtsar*) in 1 Kings 7:51 as "treasuries of the house of Yahweh."

In the Gospels, Jesus had much to say about heaven as a treasure house. Specifically, the terms that Jesus used in Matthew 6 for heaven and the treasures therein are best described in His revelation to humanity and the kingdom of heaven. The gospel writers used two Greek words, *ouranos* and *thesaurus*. These are generally translated into English as heaven and treasure, respectively. *Ouranos* speaks to heaven being both the vaulted expanse of the sky with all things visible in it and the heaven of heavens (His Father's house—see John 14:2).

The first heaven has to do with the aerial heavens or sky; this is the place where birds and airplanes fly. We know it as Earth's atmosphere. According to the Center for Science Education, the atmosphere is a mixture of gases that surrounds our planet. On Earth, the atmosphere helps make life possible. Besides providing us with the air we breathe, it shields us from most of the harmful ultraviolet (UV) radiation coming from the sun, warms the surface of our planet by about 33° C (59° F), and largely prevents extreme differences between daytime and nighttime temperatures.[15] It is the region where the clouds and the tempests gather and where thunder and lightning are produced. The second heaven holds the remainder of our solar system, galaxy, and universe. The third heaven, or "Father's house," is the region above the visible heavens. Jesus taught heaven is an eternal and spiritual dimension where His eternal God and Father dwells with His created heavenly beings.

The word *thesaurus* (treasure) speaks of the location where good and precious things are collected and laid up. Heaven is a treasury, repository, magazine, safe, and vault in which eternal valuables are kept, and the development of life in Christ begins.

Heaven is a place or vault where spiritual valuables are laid up and kept. Therefore, heaven is a place or vault where spiritual valuables are laid up and kept, as well as where Christ Jesus now resides and the redeemed who are seated in Him. In speaking to a rich young ruler who asked what it would take to become spiritually complete, Jesus said, "You still lack one thing. Sell everything you have and give to the poor, and you will have treasure in heaven. Then come, follow me" (Luke 18:22, NIV).

And when encouraging His disciples, Jesus said,

> *Do not be afraid, little flock, for your Father has been pleased to give you the kingdom. Sell your possessions and give to the poor. Provide purses for yourselves that will not wear out, a treasure in heaven that will never*

fail, where no thief comes near and no moth destroys.
For where your treasure is, there your heart will be also.

— Luke 12:32–34 (NIV)

I love what Albert Barnes said concerning the treasure house of heaven. He said,

> *In heaven nothing corrupts; nothing terminates; no*
> *enemies plunder or destroy. To have treasure in heaven*
> *is to possess evidence that its purity and joys will be*
> *ours. It is to be heirs of God, and joint heirs with*
> *Christ, to an inheritance incorruptible, undefiled,*
> *and that fades not away (see 1 Peter 1:4). The heart,*
> *or affections, will of course be fixed on the treasure. To*
> *regulate the heart, it is therefore important that the*
> *treasure, or object of attachment, should be right.*[16]

From all of this, it is important to see that heaven is a real place. Heaven is the eternal home of Almighty God, and it is Him that must come first and foremost in our lives. Heaven is the first place of God's light, and His light continues to fill heaven. Our hearts must be devoted to and be filled with God's light. With He and the light of heaven as our aim, our lives will turn to focus on accessing the treasures of heaven for the sake of sharing that light with the world. By being filled with God's light, our heart is assured of having everything we need for life and godliness. We know beyond our natural understanding that through our Father and Savior, all is well, both in life and death. As bestselling author Randy Alcorn said,

Set your hearts on things above, where Christ is seated
at the right hand of God" (Colossians 3:1). This is
a direct command to set our hearts on the things of
heaven. And to make sure we don't miss the importance
of a heaven-centered life, the next verse says, "Set your
minds on things above, not on earthly things."[17]

CHAPTER FOUR:

Exporting Treasure to Earth

For the Son of Man came to seek and to save the lost.

— Luke 19:10 (NIV)

In the beginning, God created the heavens and the earth. After creating all the wonders of the invisible and visible heavens, God turned His attention to creating the earth and the creation of His most precious and treasured creation, mankind. In Genesis 1:27 (NIV), it says that "God created mankind in his own image." This act of creation is described as the result of special deliberation on the part of God—the divine being or trinity taking counsel with Himself in the matter (verse 26). Mankind, therefore, did not evolve from apes, as Darwin theorized, but mankind was created as God's most treasured creation, formed, fashioned, shaped out of "earth," and made after the "image of God." This means men and women were created to be God's stewards (Titus 1:7) and fellow laborers with God (1 Corinthians 3:9).[18]

Man's destiny was to "replenish the earth, and subdue it: and have dominion over the fish of the sea, and over the fowl of the air, and over every living thing" (Genesis 1:28, KJV). In other words, mankind was and is the central piece of God's plan for exporting the treasures of heaven to the earth, and there is no backup plan.

By the eternal God's divine interjection of His breath, Adam became a "living soul" (Hebrew: *nephesh chayyah*). This is a reference to the breath of life (or lives—Hebrew: *nishmath chayyim*) being breathed into Adam by the Eternal God. Adam became God's *treasure chest* on the earth. In that first Adam, God put His most valuable treasure, Himself (His own eternal Spirit).

With His Spirit came His light, life, and love, as well as the attributes of peace, goodness, gentleness, joy, and self-determination (just to name a few). This act of God provided Adam with a special relationship with God. He was made different than all the heavenly hosts of angels. Instead of being created as a servant, Scripture says Adam was created as a *son of God*. When God exported Himself and the treasures of heaven into Adam, He was not looking to form a religion but to forge a relationship. He wanted a relationship with beings that were made in His likeness and who were given a free choice to either love or not love Him.

Adam was created as a son of God.

God breathed into Adam, and the man literally *came to life*. Adam was special and unique. He was placed within a new and unusual garden that God had planted in the east (Genesis 2:8, 15–17). The Garden of Eden was the place of Adam's original work and purpose, but most of all, Eden was a meeting place where God walked and talked with Adam. In Eden, God communicated His words, His will, and ways with Adam concerning all creation. And Adam spoke dynamically, naming each animal, bird, and fish, as well as all the other parts of God's creation. What a glorious beginning for mankind! God gave only one commandment. He warned Adam that his disobedience would bring about an end to heaven on Earth, "You are free to eat from any tree in the garden; but you must not eat from the tree of the knowledge of good and evil, for when you eat of it you will surely die" (Genesis 2:16–17, NIV).

The Bible does not tell us how much time passed before God saw that it was not good for Adam to be alone. We do know that God saw that Adam was alone and formed him a suitable helper out of Adam's own body (verses 18–21). Using one of Adam's ribs, the Lord made a woman (called Eve by Adam). And again, we do not know how days, weeks, years, centuries, or even millennia Adam and Eve lived in the Garden, being with and communicating with God. It must have been a wonderful time. In that wondrous place created by God, the treasures of heaven were fully transported to Earth. In that place, there was no sin, sadness, sickness, or suffering. It truly was heaven on Earth. And in both Adam and Eve, love, peace, righteousness, and joy reigned supreme.

The Bible tells us that there came a time when Adam allowed himself to be deceived and made the fateful decision to commit treason by willfully disobeying the instructions given to him by God. Simply put, his disobedience caused Adam and all his descendants to be robbed of God's eternal valuables, beginning with God's light. Through Adam's disobedience, sin entered the world, bringing separation from God and the world's plunge into spiritual darkness. Theologians define sin as disobedience to the law of God. Primarily sin is seen as an act, but it is actually an act founded on an immoral decision. *In other words, Adam decided to sin before committing the sin.*

From the very moment sin entered the world, sin affected and afflicted mankind in the most terrible ways. The effects of sin are not only seen in the outward world of created things and persons but also in and upon the person who commits the act of sin.[19] It isn't merely the actual commission of the sin. But like the sin of adultery, which in itself is sin, adultery begins with the thought and intent of lustful desire, which eventually leads to evil thought, imagination, and, ultimately, the act itself. Premeditated murder is not merely the actual killing of a person; it is the spirit of hatred which makes the thought of murder welcome (Matthew 5:21, 27). Therefore, sin robbed Adam and his descendants of being the place where God stored His most precious spiritual valuables of light, life, and love, as well as the fruit of a righteous life. These are listed in Galatians 5:22–23 as the fruit of the Spirit (joy, peace, patience, kindness, goodness, faithfulness, gentleness, and self-control).

Because of sin, mankind also lost the ability to have a full and complete relationship with his creator. Once this relationship was disconnected, spiritual understanding was lost. The apostle Paul referred to this in 1 Corinthians 2:14 (NIV),

> *The person without the Spirit does not accept the things that come from the Spirit of God but considers them foolishness, and cannot understand them because they are discerned only through the Spirit.*

The reason the natural man cannot discern spiritual things is that the loss of spiritual discernment is the result of the human race losing its spiritual light and sight. Once the sight is lost, what remains is spiritual blindness. Spiritual deliverance and the subsequent illumination needed for salvation, sanctification, and service can only be provided by the Holy Spirit. How can we obtain such light? We must first accept God's plan of salvation for ourselves.

Here is a short version of that plan. In the fullness of time, the last Adam, the Lord Jesus Christ, came to Earth, lived a sinless life, and gave His life on the cross to redeem mankind. His sacrificial death and subsequent resurrection opened the opportunity for all men and women to be redeemed from the curse of sin and to have the penalty, power, and presence of sin removed from their lives. Such wondrous salvation provides the only way for one to have heaven's light and restored understanding. This occurs as the Holy Spirit takes up residence within the heart of every believer! Hallelujah! By coming to the saving knowledge of Jesus Christ, which includes the repenting of sin and embracing Christ Jesus as Savior and Lord, we become the holy temple, the habitation, the dwelling place, and the home of the Holy Spirit on the earth.

Salvation provides us a way to be God's treasure chest on the earth and to possess the eternal deposit of the Holy Spirit (more valuable than anything the natural world can offer or comprehend). Paul described this as having "treasure in earthen vessels" (2 Corinthians 4:7, KJV). Our regeneration in Christ Jesus makes us a new creation. The old has passed away. Everything has become new! By grace through faith, we who believe have been redeemed, made sons and daughters of God, and filled with His glorious light as well as the blessing and splendid eternal riches of God.

Therefore, we (the redeemed) are now spiritually seated in the place of honor (at the right of the Father) in Christ Jesus, in the heavenlies (Ephesians 1:3). It is our being placed in that spiritual location that speaks to the value God has placed on us and within each of us. In other words, God's most valued treasure and treasure chest is now *us*! We must embrace the value God has placed in and on us as well as seek to discover all of His wonderful treasures. Jesus said such are to be experienced, embraced, enjoyed, and then be stored in heaven, where thieves cannot steal or rust and mold destroy. Simply put, God wants each of us to *learn how to embrace and enjoy His life!*

As I stated earlier, God wanted a family of sons and daughters who would be in communion with Him and would fulfill the purpose for which He had created them. Since Adam's fall, most people have sought to understand the reason for their lives, and like so many today, you may be reading this book because you are searching for the answer to the question; why am I here?

For most of us, questions like this generally begin bubbling to the surface as the innocence of childhood begins to fade. As we finish the different stages of our life, the question arises again and again. It seems that most of the decisions in our young adult life call from within and without examining, estimating, and experiencing our potential and purpose. For most people, there is a need to find an answer that will satisfy their soul. For others, the answers they find seem to only last for a particular season and are found to be subject to continuous examination and speculation. This is especially true if the decisions we make as young adults do not bring about the results we were hoping for or expecting. Then more questions arise, only to be followed by even more questions in our mid-life and elderly years.

Why is the answer to this question so difficult for so many people today? I believe there has become a lack of spiritual light (understanding) either in or untapped by most people. Many contemporary Christians have lost the hunger to hear from God for themselves and have turned toward looking to or requesting information from the internet or their friends for answers. Many have chosen this route rather than relying on the wisdom of those who have gone before them or the spiritual gifts Christ has set in His church (Ephesians 4). This kind of thinking is like a baseball asking itself (if it were possible) or another baseball for the reason why baseballs were created in the first place. I have no doubt that some baseballs (if they could talk) would say they were created to be thrown, while others were made to be caught, hit, or fielded. And some would probably say they were made to be autographed and admired.

But like a baseball, any person or thing that has been created cannot fully define the purpose or potential of their own creation. Such thinking is the basis for deception and the creation of idols. Noah Webster defines an idol as anything on which we set our affections, that to which we indulge an excessive and sinful attachment. He also said an *idol* is anything that usurps the place of God in the hearts of His rational creatures.[20]

In other words, an idol is nothing more than something imagined by a person that is used to define or determine God's purpose or potential for that person or other human beings. This includes everything else God created. In the Old Testament, it was the ministry of the prophet that God used on most occasions to confront the worship of idols. And now the church is desperately again in great need of dynamic prophetic ministry! Why?

The purpose of a person or thing can only be found in the mind of the creator of that person or thing. Too many humans assume to know how to use a modern invention by only knowing a few of the basics, taking information off the internet, watching an online video, or by their own experience. Such people do not usually take the time to examine what was in the mind of the creator or even the manufacturer who produced it. Only the creator of a thing can rightly define and describe the complete purpose and potential of that thing. It is the creator who had the original idea prior to that thing being created and manufactured, as well as the limitations and possibilities that would cause the best use of the creation. Such use would cause the creation to accomplish its fullest potential.

When a buyer does not consult the information contained within the owner's mind, they assume to know the purpose of a thing without seeking out the idea put in motion by the creator or the limits and full potential established by the manufacturer. This lack of action does two things. First, it gives the possibility to the thing being misused, and it limits the potential of the equipment to the opinion or experiences of the buyer.

David said, "The earth is the LORD's, and everything in it, the world, and all who live in it" (Psalm 24:1, NIV). One of the distinctive characteristics of God as creator is that He is the conceiver, creator, and completer of the universe. That means He conceived, created, and completed each of us! He conceived us, not simply in our present form or state, but from the beginning and prior to anything existing but Him (Genesis 1:1). He proceeded to create everything on the whole earth (including us) and desires to complete everything for His intended purpose. In other words, He is seeking to develop each of us into that which He chose and called us to be.

Accepting the concept of God's cause, creation, and proprietorship of our lives first means we have been made in His likeness (image) and that our existence is because of Him. He did not create us without potential or purpose. Therefore, it is important for us to open ourselves to the prophetic Spirit of God so that we might know the mind of Christ and what He planned for us to become before the beginning began. Endless opportunities have been planned and can be found in Him. He is the one who knows the limits of our potential (because He knows what we truly believe about Him and ourselves).

It is important for us to open ourselves to the prophetic Spirit of God.

Therefore, our purpose can only be fully understood by the information provided to us by the creator and manufacturer (God), His Word (the owner's manual revealed fully in Christ), and the Holy Spirit's ministry. The precepts and principles set forth in His Word provide information and illustration, but it is the work of the Holy Spirit that illuminates and reveals. In his letter to the Ephesians, Paul prayed that,

> *The God of our Lord Jesus Christ, the glorious Father, may give you the Spirit of wisdom and revelation, so that you may know him better. I pray that the eyes of your heart may be enlightened in order that you may know the hope to which he has called you, the riches of his glorious inheritance in his holy people, and his incomparably great power for us who believe.*
>
> — Ephesians 1:17–19 (NIV)

As the creator and owner of the heavens and the earth, as well as everyone and thing within them, God has a legal right and exclusive title to our lives. He is the One who works the raw materials of our gifts, talents, abilities, and calling into a life suitable for His use and enables us to accomplish His good work, thus fulfilling our purpose and enabling us to reach our full potential. By the gift of God and the fulfillment of our purpose, we are to become the *proprietors* of the earth and made valuable as to the fulfillment of God's creation and the transformation of the society in which we live.

Again, a person's purpose is found in the original intent for the creation of that person. The original intent can only be found in the mind of the creator. Another creation (person) cannot know the potential and purpose of your life! You are God-created, and your purpose can only be defined and established by God. Nothing that God has said about our lives or has put into our lives is without purpose.

Our full value (becoming and being one of God's treasure chests in this place called Earth) is determined by our willingness to embrace the purpose for which we were born. This journey begins when we accept Jesus Christ as our Lord and Savior. It is He who redeemed us from the curse, removed our sins, and restored heaven's valuables of righteousness, peace, and joy to our lives. We have become the temple of the Holy Spirit. We are God's vault on the earth and have an eternal deposit that the world did not give and cannot take away. We have been created to house the blessing and riches of God. By doing so, we have been put on the road to living a very blessed life and becoming a blessing to others.

Let me say it again; we earthlings are valuable because we have been created by God and for God. We came from Him and, as believers, have been seated in heavenly places in and with Christ Jesus. I believe one of the best ways to understand our value, purpose, and potential is found again in Paul's letter to the Ephesians.

Praise be to the God and Father of our Lord Jesus Christ, who has blessed us in the heavenly realms with every spiritual blessing in Christ. For he chose us in him before the creation of the world to be holy and blameless in his sight. In love he predestined us for adoption to sonship through Jesus Christ.

— Ephesians 1:3–5 (NIV)

I keep asking that the God of our Lord Jesus Christ, the glorious Father, may give you the Spirit of wisdom and revelation, so that you may know him better. I pray that the eyes of your heart may be enlightened in order that you may know the hope to which he has called you, the riches of his glorious inheritance in his holy people, and his incomparably great power for us who believe. That power is the same as the mighty strength he exerted when he raised Christ from the dead and seated him at his right hand in the heavenly realms, far above all rule and authority, power and dominion, and every name that is invoked, not only in the present age but also in the one to come.

— Ephesians 1:17–21 (NIV)

Let's review before we move on. A redeemed man or woman is the chest where God desires to place His valuables. Adam, the first man, was robbed of the valuables through deception, decision, and the destructive forces of sin. But, the last Adam, the Lord Jesus Christ, has restored a way for heaven's valuables to be replaced, replenished, and restored. Those who have accepted the Lord Jesus as the Savior are now positioned in Christ, in heavenly places, and are God's treasure chest, designed to house God's valuables or riches.

> *And God raised us up with Christ and seated us with him in the heavenly realms in Christ Jesus, in order that in the coming ages he might show the incomparable riches of his grace, expressed in his kindness to us in Christ Jesus.*
>
> — Ephesians 2:6–7 (NIV)

Jesus taught this concept when He taught His disciples to pray in Matthew 6:9–10 (NIV), "This, then, is how you should pray: 'Our Father in heaven, hallowed be your name, your kingdom come, your will be done, on earth as it is in heaven.'"

Because we are made in the image of God, have a deposit of the Holy Spirit, and are made to be living souls, our value to God is incomprehensible. I also believe that there are specific values or treasures that God wants us to embrace, expand, and enjoy for the sake of increasing our value to His kingdom and to the people around us.

If we are going to embrace the coming restoration and manifestation of prophetic knowledge, wisdom, and understanding, the process must begin by:

- Learning to fully love God and others.
- Having a renewed mind.
- Implementing and maintaining an attitude of gratitude.
- Living a life full of faith.
- Acquiring a balance between humility and confidence.
- Blessing and generously serving others.
- Fostering our full potential, as well as living a purpose and focused life.

These are the values and treasures Jesus referenced in His Sermon on the Mount. All of them were deposited into Adam and then lost through original sin. Thankfully, by Jesus giving His life on the cross and His subsequent resurrection, they all have been restored to every believer at salvation. Whether or not we choose to be fully illuminated to them or institute and develop them is greatly determined by our willingness to embrace personal spiritual development. It is His will that these treasures of heaven be continually developed with ever-increasing dimensions of glory within us. Paul described this as Christ living in and through us, the hope of glory.

CHAPTER FIVE:

The Prophetic Expression of Heavenly Treasures

But as many as received him, to them gave he power to become the sons of God, even to them that believe on his name: Which were born, not of blood, nor of the will of the flesh, nor of the will of man, but of God.

— John 1:12–13 (KJV)

Once you clearly recognize and choose to live effectively in Christ, you won't try to operate out of your old nature. But rather, the Holy Spirit will begin to manifest His nature in your life. The word manifest comes from the Greek word *phaneroo*. The word means to make visible or known what has been hidden or unknown, whether by words, deeds, or in any other way. How does such occur? As the Holy Spirit shines His light out from within our lives, His power is expressed both in and through us. Paul said it would be "according to the power that worketh in us" (Ephesians 3:20b, KJV). Because we are sons and daughters of God, we don't simply work for God like a servant, but rather He works in and through us as His children and representatives on Earth. When Jesus Christ came to live within us by the Holy Spirit, He deposited all the power of the Godhead bodily in us (see Colossians 2:9).

This means we have been given a new nature. We are new creatures. We can do all things through Christ Jesus! We have the power to overcome all obstacles and to live a life full of Him! Hallelujah! Sadly, many identify and operate out of what they see and who they used to be. Sadly, for many people, the idea of living a life full of and led by the Holy Spirit seems extreme. Here is an illustration of the steps that are needed for us to implement the process that enables us both to realize our potential and fulfill our purpose. Hint: start at the bottom of the illustration.

RESULTS
Encountering, Embracing and Enjoying the
Prophetic and Hidden Treasures in Christ

ACTIONS AND HABITS
The Manifestation of Our Attitudes,
Convictions, and Values

 WORDS
Prophetic Expression of Christ in Us,
the Hope of Glory

SPIRITUAL VALUES
Humility, Confidence, Honor, Submission

 CONVICTIONS
The Bedrock and Reward of Faith

ATTITUDE
Positive or Negative.
Is Gratitude Our Attitude?

 TRANSFORMATION OF OUR MIND
How We See God, His Word, Ourselves, and Others

GOD WITHIN
A Heart Filled with God and His Love

Our lives should be summed up in what the apostle Paul told the Romans, "For whom he did foreknow [that is us], he also did predestinate to be conformed to the image of his Son, that he might be the firstborn among many brethren" (Romans 8:29, KJV).

When did God foreknow us? From and in eternity (Ephesians 1:14). What did He do? Appointed us beforehand as in Acts 4:28 and 1 Corinthians 2:7. To become what? *Conformed to and to acquire the likeness, similarity, resemblance, and image (which is the very representation, picture, illustration, and prototype of the Son of God).* Who is He? The Lord Jesus Christ, Himself. He is Messiah, king, wonderful, mighty God, and Immanuel! He also is the firstborn or the *pattern* for those who are His brethren (that's us!), and now the creation waits in eager expectation for the sons of God (again, that's us) to be revealed (Romans 8:19).

There is a sharp distinction between those persons who with those who speak "out of their own heart" versus the people who watch their words and are not looking to speak out of their own originated reflection or calculation. Such is generally a product of a person's feelings, fears, or hopes. We must seek to possess and convey the heart, mind, and attitude of Christ (Galatians 2:20). For such to occur, it is not necessary that we hear the literal voice of God (heard phonetically through our natural ear). His voice is generally heard and distinguished in knowing His Word or as His soft still voice spoken from within our regenerated spirit (personal consciousness and understanding).

Because the Spirit of God acts with full freedom, He can select and make known His voice according to His will to every person with no respect to race (Romans 1:16), age (1 Samuel 3:4), or gender (Judges 4:4).

Having and speaking the mind of Christ involves more than human reason. Our human mind must be transformed from its own finite limitations and embrace the infinite possibilities that can be found and realized in Christ. For in the fulfillment of the life, death, and resurrection of our Lord Jesus Christ, we see His perfection as the voice of God. His words bring revelation beyond the conveying of information. His words are to be experienced. Through His words, those who truly heard Him speak were both exposed to God and felt they were being called upon by God Himself.

This caused people to see and receive beyond the surface of Jesus' words and actions. They experienced Him immediately, gradually, and successively. It is through the Lord living His life in and through us (Galatians 2:20) that we can encounter the Lord as the "person" beyond the mystery we call "life." His indescribable inner Presence in us becomes a voice, disclosing that God is not a being that is apart from His people. He is not an enigma but a person full of grace, kindness, mercy, and love. Jesus is not only the king to which we are accountable but also the pattern for our lives. He does not have to be an "unknown" God. He is our Savior and Lord. He is our friend and brother, the God of Abraham, who, out of the endless ages, comes with compassion and guidance.

> *Jesus is not only the king to which we are accountable but also the pattern for our lives.*

The best example of this that I know in Scripture is Jesus speaking about *streams of living water flowing in, through, and from our lives.*

> *On the last and greatest day of the festival, Jesus stood and said in a loud voice, "Let anyone who is thirsty come to me and drink. Whoever believes in me, as the Scripture has said, rivers of living water will flow from within them." By this he meant the Spirit, whom those who believed in him were later to receive. Up to that time the Spirit had not been given, since Jesus had not yet been glorified.*
>
> — John 7:37–39 (NIV)

In this passage, Jesus used water to illustrate the moving of the Holy Spirit in the life of the believer. What do we know about water? Water's first property is that it is fluid, and therefore water can move or flow. When water moves or flows, it always follows the path of least resistance. And as it flows, its tendency is to widen, deepen, and purify. Water can also change direction. In Ezekiel chapter forty-seven, the prophet watched as water flowed out from the throne of God, under the threshold of the temple, and became a river. He saw the water deepen. Its depth started at the ankles, moved to the knees, loins, and then there was water to swim in. The deeper and swifter a river flows, the greater its power to move things and take those things to a different place that from where those things were encountered by the river. A river also produces life within itself, for the creatures who live in it, along its bank, and to all that are touched by or choose to access it.

From these and other scriptures, we know that the words and actions of a deepening life in Christ can be likened to this illustration. As Christ's life fills us to the point of overflow, His Presence flows from the throne of our heart (where God is seated) with humility, confidence, honor, submission, and a commitment to service. His life flows in humility from "under the threshold" of His plans and purposes. Over time, the river of life grows deeper and wider. It brings light and life to the individual from whence it flows, to those nearby, and to everyone they meet. Others can drink from that life and taste God's goodness, grace, and glory.

When such a person joins with others of precious faith, the one life and stream becomes a tributary that comes together with other lives. This results in more people being encouraged, touched, saved, healed, and blessed! The streams together then become a river that moves the debris of darkness and sin from society. This same river brings righteousness, joy, and peace (i.e., the kingdom of God) to everyone and everything it encounters. Praise the Name of the Lord!

CHAPTER SIX:

Treasured, Chosen, and Valued

*Praise be to the God and Father of our Lord Jesus
Christ, who has blessed us in the heavenly realms with
every spiritual blessing in Christ. For he chose us in
him before the creation of the world to be holy and
blameless in his sight.*

— Ephesians 1:3–4 (NIV)

What comes to mind when you hear the words treasured and chosen? These are remarkably interesting words. Webster defined chosen as being selected from a number; picked out; distinguished in preference; elected; predestinated; eminent; designated to office. When we examine the word in Paul's letter to the Ephesians, we find that it is translated from the Greek word *eklegomai*. Strong's Concordance defines the word as picked or chosen out for oneself as one being chosen out of many.[21] An example is Jesus choosing His twelve apostles out of all of His disciples. It also speaks to God choosing whom He judged fit to receive His favor and separating them from the rest of mankind for the purpose of being peculiarly His own and being attended continually by His gracious oversight (the Israelites and Christians). Both are whom He set apart from the irreligious multitude as dear unto Himself and whom He has rendered, through faith in Christ, citizens in the Messianic kingdom (James 2:5) so that the ground of choice lies in Christ and His merits only.

Let's look at the root words that make up the verb *eklegomai*. The prefix of the word is *ek*, which is a primary preposition denoting origin (the point whence action or motion proceeds), from, out of place, time, or cause. It can be literal or figurative. It is from this preposition that we get the word exit. An exit is a doorway out of a place. Wherever we go, whether we are in the store, a church, or a school, the word "exit" stands over the door. Paul's use of this preposition speaks to us being "chosen out of" a place of origin with both purpose and cause.

The remainder of *eklegomai* is from the verb *lego*. We know the word because of the famous toy manufacturer. The LEGO website says the company was founded in 1932 by Ole Kirk Kristiansen, and based on the iconic LEGO brick, which is one of the world's leading manufacturers of play materials. In our world, LEGOs are toys of different shapes and sizes that are individually chosen by children to be put together for the purpose of building things.

The Greek verb *lego* comes from the noun *logos*. The apostle John, who is the author of the fourth Gospel, used the word *Logos* to define the eternal existence and Person of the Lord Jesus. His Gospel is not, however, the first New Testament writer who represents Jesus as such. Though Paul does not actually use the word in this way, I believe he understood the Johannine concept.

Christ is represented by Paul as before His advent living a life with God in heaven (Galatians 4:4; Romans 10:6). He is presented as the One in whose image earthly beings, and especially men, were made (1 Corinthians 15:45–49); and even as participating in the creation (1 Corinthians 8:6). And, in virtue of His distinct being, Paul calls Jesus God's "own Son" (Romans 8:32).[22]

That would mean that we, from the eternal Logos (Word of God), were chosen from Him, chosen for Him, and chosen by Him so that we could be fitly put together in Him. When did He choose us? Before the creation or foundation of the world. Before we arrived on the planet, we had already been chosen. We may have come to the saving knowledge of Him as broken people, but before we existed, we were unbroken in Him. And, by believing in and embracing His death, burial, and resurrection, He is refitting us together as we were before the beginning began. David spoke of this in Psalm 139:13–16 (NIV),

Before we arrived on the planet, we had already been chosen.

> *For you created my inmost being; you knit me together in my mother's womb. I praise you because I am fearfully and wonderfully made; your works are wonderful, I know that full well. My frame was not hidden from you when I was made in the secret place, when I was woven together in the depths of the earth. Your eyes saw my unformed body; all the days ordained for me were written in your book before one of them came to be.*

The pieces of our lives are being put back together. Wherever you are in life, know this, God is not finished with you yet! He is still working all things out for your good! I'm speaking not just for our good as individuals, but He is working to connect each of us to those that will see and acknowledge our value as well as those that we will see value in as well. He is connecting each of us to the people we need in our lives. Why? He has designs on us (together) being His masterpiece. Hallelujah!

I know some of you reading this book do not feel like a masterpiece or even look at yourself as one. That is because you have not understood the treasures that are within you or just how valuable you are to Him as well as to those whom He has, is, and will connect you to. Perhaps, when your elementary teacher picked captains to choose teams to play a game of kickball, softball, or basketball, you were chosen last or not chosen at all. Perhaps, a parent told you that you would never be one of Hollywood's "beautiful people" or chosen to play on an NFL team. But you were chosen from Him, in Him, and for Him. Chosen for blessing, chosen for greatness! Let me say it again, you were chosen from the beginning out of Him, by Him, for Him, and in Him, so that He could reveal His prophetic and glorious light through you! Solomon understood this. He said,

> *I know that everything God does will endure forever;*
> *nothing can be added to it and nothing taken from it.*
> *God does it so that men will fear him. Whatever is has*
> *already been, and what will be has been before; and*
> *God will call the past to account.*
>
> — Ecclesiastes 3:14–15 (NIV)

Everything that is (that includes you) has been before. Where were you? In Him. He conceived of you, your life, as well as the people and situations you are connected to. This all happened prior to the creation of the world. Before God stepped out on nothing and spoke something into existence, He knew you! Before time began, you were conceived in Him. When God created the heavens and the earth, you were there in Him! Jesus shared this same concept when He spoke to the Pharisees in John 8:56–58 (NIV),

> *"Your father Abraham rejoiced at the thought of seeing my day; he saw it and was glad."*
>
> *"You are not yet fifty years old,"* the Jews said to him, *"and you have seen Abraham!"*
>
> *"Very truly I tell you,"* Jesus answered, *"before Abraham was born, I am!"*

Apparently, the Lord knew us before time and saw us as having a very valuable place in His kingdom. To better understand this, I want you to remember who told you about the saving grace of God and how that person was brought by His providence to you in the right place and at the right time. This is due to their steps being ordered by the Lord (Psalm 37:23, NKJV). That person was, is, and will always be connected to you. Like two LEGO pieces, God put you two together. And not only has the Lord accomplished this to bring you initially to Him, but your life in Him continues to be connected to those He chose you to be connected to before the beginning of time began.

The best illustration I know is from the word *logos* or Word. The pre-incarnate Lord Jesus is *the Word*. Each of us are words that originated in Him. We are the words in His book. Altogether He is and came as the volume of the book (Hebrews 10:7). In Him, we are His words in His book. His book is His-story! Therefore, we are a word (small case) in the Word (large case).

Each of us is one of the eight parts of speech. We are either nouns, pronouns, verbs, adjectives, adverbs, prepositions, interjections, or conjunctions. God has put us in a specific sentence, paragraph, page, and chapter in His book. My pastor friend, Lon McVeigh, like most pastors, is a conjunction. Whether Lon is at the grocery store, church, or the mall, he is connecting to and with people. He connects people to the message of Christ. He connects his congregation to missionaries who minister in faraway countries. He connects with everyone he meets and does his best to see that they are connected to Christ.

I believe my wife is, more than likely, an adjective. Adjectives are words that modify. She is always modifying others. Her special calling is to children. She is both a wonderful mom and teacher. Her heart is to modify the beliefs, attitudes, and actions of those she teaches. She even does her best to modify me! Her desire is for everyone she meets to love the Lord Jesus, to know Him, and to modify their behavior so as to conform to the Word of God.

You are an individual, chosen by God and called according to His purpose.

You are not a clone. You are an individual, chosen by God and called according to His purpose.

You are seen by Him as exceptional, valuable, and unique. Your place in His-story and life holds a distinctive position in His book. You are a special word. You have been placed within a specific sentence, paragraph, and chapter. He has chosen you to be in Christ so that you add value to everyone that is on the same page as you are. It is so important for us to realize how valuable each of us really is.

Before the beginning of time, there was a meeting. In that meeting was God the Father, God the Son, and God the Holy Spirit. The Father thought you; the Son (Word) spoke you, and the Holy Spirit has placed you in Christ Jesus. You are now being put together with those to whom you have been called and chosen. Paul wrote to the Romans that by their faith in Christ, they received the spirit of adoption, "The Spirit you received brought about your adoption to sonship. And by him we cry, 'Abba, Father.' The Spirit himself testifies with our spirit that we are God's children" (Romans 8:15–16, NIV).

When did God decide to adopt us? Before the beginning began. When was our name written in heaven's book? Before the beginning began. (Not when we were saved.) What happened the day we were saved? We agreed with God's decision to adopt us! In our agreement, He issued a new birth certificate that certifies we are His!

Let me tell you a story about my own family that will illustrate my point. Several years ago, Susan and I adopted a baby boy. According to the laws of the state we lived in at the time, the birth mother had to agree to the adoption twice, first when the baby was born and again six months later. Everything went well the first time. But, six months later, she did not show up to finalize the adoption. Our attempt to locate her was to no avail. Almost five years went by, there was no contact, and the adoption of our son was not finalized. We appealed to the state where we lived, and it was determined that on his fifth birthday, the court could and would issue the final adoption decree—if our son agreed to the adoption (in front of a judge).

So, on his fifth birthday, our whole family went to the courthouse. As we stood before the judge, he asked each family member: me, my wife, and our two daughters, if we agreed to adopt our son. What a question! Our decision had already been made! We had raised him for almost five years! And, of course, our answer was yes! The judge turned to our son and asked him. Our son also said yes! He wanted to be adopted, and he agreed to us being his family! The judge hit his gavel on his desk and decreed that the adoption was final! Our son was finally, totally, and completely, as well as legally, our son.

But that was not the end of the story! A month later, on my birthday, we received our son's new birth certificate in the mail. The judge had gone back in time five years and reissued his birth certificate. On the new one, my wife and I were listed as his birth parents. In other words, what the judge did was declare that our son was ours from his very beginning! Hallelujah!

When we made the decision to come to Christ and trust Him for salvation, we simply agreed to the decision He had made before time began. He had already adopted us (as far as He was concerned). He was reaching out to us, leading us, and guiding us to a place where we were asked by the Holy Spirit to make a decision. When we said yes to Him, everything changed. Now our past is gone! All things have become new! We have been His from the very beginning!

"Therefore, if anyone is in Christ, he is a new creation; old things have passed away; behold, all things have become new" (2 Corinthians 5:17, NKJV).

This means we are chosen and valued! We have been purchased with the precious blood of the Lamb of God. There is no price that can compare to the price our Lord and Savior paid for our salvation. He chose us from the beginning and finalized our adoption when we agreed to His plan and purpose for our lives! What a wonderful story to tell the nations! How could we ever consider having an inferiority complex? We are God's most treasured possession and have been fully adopted into His family as His heirs and joint heirs with Jesus Christ!

CHAPTER SEVEN:

Chosen and Blessed

Praise be to the God and Father of our Lord Jesus Christ, who has blessed us in the heavenly realms with every spiritual blessing in Christ.

— Ephesians 1:3 (NIV)

I simply love this verse of Scripture. It is one of my favorites and has been so for over fifty years. Why? Because the blessing mentioned is in the past tense. And like the word chosen, the word has the Greek noun *logos* as its base. The blessing of God upon our lives is not based on our performance as Christians. The blessing was determined and destined to be ours before we agreed to His decision to adopt us into His family. Our acceptance of the Lord Jesus Christ as our Savior has enabled the blessing to take root, grow and manifest both in and through us. Jesus Christ is the author (before the beginning began) and finisher (until the very end) of the Father's blessing upon our lives.

You may be asking, if this is true, why am I going through this difficult time with my health, finances, or relationships? Why is the church losing people to the things of the world? I have previously addressed Him at length as the author and the work accomplished before time. Let's now look at the finished work of Christ.

Hebrews 12:2 (NKJV) says, "Looking unto Jesus, the author and finisher of our faith, who for the joy that was set before Him endured the cross, despising the shame, and has sat down at the right hand of the throne of God." The word *finisher* is translated from the Greek word *teleiotes*. Strong's Concordance defines the word as "a perfector or one who has in his own person raised faith to its perfection and so set before us the highest example of faith." *In other words, Jesus is the pioneer of personal faith and the* teleiotes *(which is a word apparently coined by the writer from* teleioô*) or consummator of our faith.*[23]

And now, He has sat down in heaven (Greek: *kekathiken*), which is the perfect active indicative of *kathizô*, at God's right hand and still is there (1:3).[24] Our salvation is a finished work, as far as God is concerned. We humans living in the realm of time are still being worked in, on, and through by the Holy Spirit. His purpose is to finish and finalize His finished work in our lives. Whatever you may be facing, it is being used for your good. He is working to make both the positive and negative events of your life altogether lovely. For He has chosen to bless and complete you in Him. He desires to make you into the person He knew you to be before the beginning began.

Whatever you may be facing, it is being used for your good.

Consider the wonderful, optimistic, joyous, and glorious declaration, "Blessed us in the heavenly realms with every spiritual blessing in Christ" (Ephesians 1:3, NIV). This phrase speaks to the very center of our life in Christ. Where did this blessing take place? In heaven. God declares us blessed from heaven and has blessed us by moving us progressively from revelation to revelation, from faith to faith, and from glory to glory. His declaration originated in heavenly places where we are now seated (in the finished work) in Christ Jesus. Now by the Spirit, I see Him opening new aspects (of His finished work) on the earth. Why? He is finishing His finished work in you and the earth.

I love what Alexander MacLaren says concerning the blessing of God upon us. He said,

> *The aim of His act of blessing is to evoke in our hearts the love that praises. We receive first, and then, moved by His mercies, we give. Our highest response to His most precious gifts is that we shall 'take the cup of salvation, and call upon the name of the Lord,' and in the depth of thankful and recipient hearts shall say, 'Blessed be God who hath blessed us.*[25]

The blessing of God is larger than we could ever experience individually. God has blessed us individually by placing us corporately in the midst of others. The psalmist said, "God sets the solitary in families; He brings out those who are bound into prosperity" (Psalm 68:6, NKJV). Like a solitary and specific word in a sentence and paragraph, God has placed other words (people) in our lives and connected them to us for the purpose of encouraging, helping, and even motivating us to embrace all the blessings that God has already provided, declared, and continues to establish in our lives.

The blessing of God is larger than we could ever experience individually.

I had such a person given to my life. She was my maternal grandmother. Along with my wife, children, and parents, my maternal grandmother brought great blessing and inspiration to my life and ministry. Augusta Myrtle Young was born and raised in the wide-open spaces of Texas. She was the firstborn of four children. Her father was a proud Texan from the Dallas area, and her mom, who had migrated with her family from eastern Tennessee to San Antonio, married just before World War I. After John and Ada married, they chose to move their family from the hill country to the wide-open spaces of the Texas Panhandle and the booming small town of Amarillo.

From a young age, my grandmother fell in love with her Lord and Savior, Jesus Christ, and West Texas. She loved the never-ending wide-open spaces found on the western edge of the Great Plains. She cherished her time harmonizing with her teenage friends as part of an all-girls gospel quartet. After high school, she began attending the nearby Shield of Faith Bible School. For almost two years, she, along with her singing companions, traveled all over eastern New Mexico, western Oklahoma, and southwestern Kansas, as well as the vast spaces of west Texas. They enjoyed singing and sharing the good news of the kingdom of God.

I don't know exactly when I first considered her one of my "valuables" or when I realized that she had been given to me as a word and blessing from God. I do know this; she was a wonderful gift to my life. I loved spending time at her house, going to church, and talking with her about the things of God. The value I grew to see and know of her in my life had nothing to do with her singing ability or the beautiful work she performed as a seamstress. And yes, I must admit, I loved her peach cobbler, but that was not it either. I simply valued her commitment to the Lord and her family. I knew closeup the blessing of her devotion, kindness, generosity, and love. And, when she spoke, I listened. I took her words as the prophetic encouragement or correction of God.

Never considered wealthy or educated by the world's standards, my grandmother loved the Lord Jesus Christ with all her heart, and she taught me to love Him in that same way. When Myrtle passed away, now almost twenty years ago, she left me something very valuable. Yes, of the things I inherited from my grandmother were her grandmother's quilt of the Great State of Texas, her watch, as well as other natural things. But my most valued inheritance was her heart for God, her love for music, her generosity to others, and yes, even some of her singing ability. But most of all, I inherited her love for the Word of God and her spirit of encouragement. She supported my ministry both by praying each day for me and by giving financially every month until she passed away.

I have no doubt you have people like my grandmother in your life. Perhaps they are part of your family, and you have known them for years. Or perhaps you met someone at the grocery store in what seemed to be a chance meeting, only for them to become a person valued and cherished by you. There are times when we arrive at a certain place or meet a certain person for the first time, and it feels like we have already been in that place or met that person. Think of the term *déjà vu*. Most people think of *déjà vu* as some mysterious phenomenon that takes place when a person experiences a situation that they have in some way unconsciously experienced formerly. The term itself is French and speaks to something that has been "already seen." It gives the idea that a person's present situation has been lived previously.[26]

Hundreds of people come and go into and out of our lives. Most of the time, we don't feel or sense a connection, but most of us have had the experience of something special happening out of the blue. Suddenly a man or woman just seems to appear for the purpose of God using them to bless our lives or for us to be a blessing to them. Think of Acts 3, when Peter and John came into the life of the man at the Gate Beautiful. Each time we experience such, we are having a prophetic moment in time.

I had such an event happen many years ago. I was ministering at a church in central Texas, and during the praise and worship service, a family walked in. I didn't know them, and I didn't know that this was their first time visiting that church, but I felt that I should know them or that I knew them from somewhere.

After the service, I made my way to them to introduce myself. I didn't know it at the time, but God had placed them in my life and ministry (not only for me to be a blessing to them), but so that they could be a blessing to me, my ministry, as well as tens of thousands of others. At our first meeting, I mentioned to them that I had just returned from building a mission church in Honduras and that I was planning to build a second church in a couple of months. Dwight began sharing that he had been working with an international ministry team to build churches and schools throughout the Americas and invited me to dine with them so I could share more of what the Lord had called me to.

Before my arrival at their home, I sensed the glorious manifest Presence of the Holy Spirit. Then, during the meal, I felt that *déjà vu* feeling. But it was evident that I had not met them or they me prior to that week. Dwight made his initial trip to Honduras with us and became part of my foreign missions-building team. He joined my inner circle (along with Dan and Ray), and we traveled together for many years to places like Mexico, Costa Rica, Bolivia, and Tanzania, erecting several churches and Bible schools for the glory of God. In fact, it is evident to me that the small core of a construction team was put into my life so God could accomplish His purpose and glory.

Now for many years, Dwight and Cynthia have continued to be a blessing sent from God to us. They even encouraged their extended family to support our ministry by giving funds that we used to start the church and children's ministry we pioneered in North Texas. Through the years, Susan and I have been richly blessed by our relationship with them. Our friendship and connection to them have led us into a relationship with their extended family, other pastors, churches, and people. Before the beginning began, that blessing was designed by God. He prophetically directed our steps and ministry, leading and guiding us along the way. What appeared to be a *happen chance* meeting in central Texas has changed the lives of tens of thousands of people around the world.

So, the next time your waiter or waitress comes to the table, take note. It may be a meeting like the one Jesus had with the Samaritan woman or like I have experienced dozens of times. You may not know the person you meet personally or even at all, but God does. He knows you, and He understands who He wants you to be to them and what He wants them to be to you. In short, He wants you to be blessed and to bless them.

For He decided before the beginning began that you, His chosen anointed vessel (a word spoken from His mouth), would show up in certain places and times so that someone could hear the gospel or be encouraged and helped. I have been all over the world and have walked through airports, ministered in churches, and taught in seminars and schools. In every place I am, I look for God to speak prophetically both to me and through me. No, I'm not looking to upgrade to a better airline seat or a better hotel room. I'm looking for those that God has designed for me to be in connection with (in my sentence, paragraph, and chapter of life).

Over the last several years, my Lord has connected me to many such people in Malawi, Kenya, and Tanzania. I am also linked to folks in Central and South America as well as in the Caribbean. I count each person as a special gift of God to my life. As a young man from Idaho, I never dreamed of the blessing God would put into my life. And, if He has done it for me, I know He is doing it for you. I pray you receive this prophetic word and start looking for those He wants you to be connected with. Begin praying to become someone's blessing today. You will be glad you did!

SECTION TWO:

Embracing New Spiritual Realities

Once you clearly recognize how treasured, valued, and blessed you are in Christ, you won't seek to continue to operate out of your old nature or old ways of looking at things. But rather, you will seek the Holy Spirit to manifest His will and ways both through your words and actions.

If you take the time to embrace the process I have thus far outlined in this book, His prophetic thoughts and words will increase in intensity as you abide in the Presence of God. God's Presence is revealed in Scripture through several different words, including the Hebrew word *panim*. In the Old Testament, *panim* is used for the showing or revealing of *God's face or Presence* (see Genesis 3:8; Exodus 33:14; Psalm 95:2; Isaiah 63:9). Two other words that you may be better familiar with are glory and *shekhinah*. Glory is the possession and characteristic of Yahweh and is given by Him to His people or to anything which is connected with Him. In Isaiah 60:7, the Lord promises to glorify the house of His glory, and the meaning is clearly that He will impart to His house the beauty and majesty that belong to Him. Glory is one of the qualities which are distinctive of Yahweh (1 Chronicles 29:11).[27] The other word is *Shekhinah* which means "the visible majesty of the Divine Presence or that which dwells." *Shekhinah* is from the Hebrew verb *shakhen*, or *shakhan*, meaning "to dwell" or "reside." This word is not found directly in the original text of the Bible but can be seen as revealed in Isaiah 60:2, Matthew 17:5, Luke 2:9, and Romans 9:4. *Shekhinah* speaks of God revealing His Presence and His choice to reside or dwell within us (1 Corinthians 6:19).[28]

What is the Presence of God? It is His glorious moral attributes, His infinite perfection revealed to, in, and through mankind. It denotes God's revelation of His being, nature, and charisma to all. As the Lord revealed Himself to Moses, His glorious values and character is shown through these attributes for the purpose of revealing His person. Each sacred value offered to us in this "proclamation" is important to the foundation of the values of generosity and blessing.

The words *bless* and *blessing* are found more frequently in the Old Testament than in the New Testament and are used in different types of relationships. The word *bless* comes from the Hebrew word *barakh*, and is first used in Genesis 1:22 at the introduction of animal life upon the earth, where it is written, "And God blessed them." The context furnishes the key to its meaning, which is the bestowal of good, and in this instance, the pleasure and power of increase in kind. In both Testaments, the context always establishes and reveals the character or value of bestowal; for instance (where man is the recipient), whether the good is temporal or spiritual, or both.[29]

Throughout the Bible the instances where the word *barakh* is used generally to show God the creator as the source of blessing and the creature (man and the creation) the recipient, but the order is sometimes reversed, and the creature (man) is the source and the creator, the recipient. In Genesis 24:48 (NIV), for example, Abraham's servant says, "I bowed down and worshiped the LORD. I praised [*barakh*] the LORD, the God of my master Abraham." In this instance, the word evidently means to bless, worship God, and to exalt and praise Him.[30]

There is a third use of the word *barakh*. Yes, in most instances, human beings only are considered as giving and/or receiving the blessing. But there are also instances where blessing another person may be taken in the prophetic sense, as when Isaac prophetically blessed Jacob (Genesis 27:4, 27). Here Jacob's father put himself, as it were, in God's place, and with a sense of divine concurrence, he pronounced the blessing upon his son. Here the word becomes in part a prayer for and in part a prediction (or prophecy) of the good intended.[31] Other examples of the good resulting from being blessed and blessing others are included in some of the proverbs written by Solomon.

A generous person will prosper; whoever refreshes others will be refreshed.

— Proverbs 11:25 (NIV)

The generous will themselves be blessed, for they share their food with the poor.

— Proverbs 22:9 (NIV)

It is a sin to despise one's neighbor, but blessed is the one who is kind to the needy.

— Proverbs 14:21 (NIV)

A wife of noble character who can find? She is worth far more than rubies. ...Her children arise and call her blessed; her husband also, and he praises her.

— Proverbs 31:10, 28 (NIV)

Human beings generally seek to be on the receiving end when it comes to blessings. But as Paul reiterated in his words to the Ephesian elders in Acts 20:35 (NIV), "In everything I did, I showed you that by this kind of hard work we must help the weak, remembering the words the Lord Jesus himself said: 'It is more blessed to give than to receive.'" God's ultimate purpose is for us to be joined to Him as well as other believers, called the body of Christ. Then as we and those around us begin beholding the Presence (face) of the Lord, we will and continue to be transformed into the image of God's dear Son, the Lord Jesus Christ.

God's ultimate purpose is for us to be joined to Him as well as other believers, called the body of Christ.

It is through our being generous as well as blessing the Lord and others that we discover (to our joy and amazement) that His purpose for us is to be in glorious union and fellowship with each other. It has been my experience that in such relationships, I have found that those I have been connected to (remember me stating how each of us are words in a sentence, paragraph, and chapter) have been likewise taught and trained in their individual relationships with Him. It is here I received a revelation that changed my perspective.

Let me reiterate it from a few pages ago, each of us should see ourselves as a stream or channel that God is joining with other streams (believers) for the purpose of eventually flowing together with all believers as the great river of God, which is full of water (Spirit) and will bless all humanity. It would appear then that God's perfect purpose in us embracing the new level of prophetic ministry that is about to begin is to bring about the promise given to Abraham that all the peoples of the earth would be blessed through him (see Genesis 12:1–3).

Streams flow into rivers, and rivers flow into the ocean, and from the ocean, the water rises to become clouds that bring rain upon the land. The purpose of the rain is not merely to replenish the rivers and flow back into the oceans but to *water the earth*. For beyond His generosity and blessing to our individual lives, God desires that in our coming together, He will "water the earth" that it may bring forth and bud. And after the budding, He wants the fruit, that He may give seed to the sower and bread to the eater (2 Corinthians 9:7).

So, it must be with our lives. Our ultimate purpose should be to learn to pour out His Presence in all that we say and do so that others may be healed and blessed. I ask that you stop reading and take a few minutes to meditate on the following scriptures. Ask the Lord to mold and shape your life into a new avenue of generosity and blessing to God and others. (Read Genesis 12:2; Deuteronomy 15:10–11; Luke 6:38.)

CHAPTER EIGHT:

It Begins with Your Heart

Blessed are the pure in heart, for they will see God.

— Matthew 5:8 (NIV)

The heart is more than the central organ in the body. Scripture describes the heart as the center of a human's moral, spiritual, and even intellectual life. The heart is the seat of a person's passions, emotions, and appetites. Having a heart full of the Holy Spirit will be both valuable and necessary to the move of God that is about to burst upon the earth. For you to be prepared and your life to become more effective and prophetic ministry successful, you must open your innermost being so the Holy Spirit can fill your heart to overflowing with the love of God. When we examine the lives and ministries of the most successful people in the Bible, one thing stands out; they loved God and His people with all their hearts. Such people took this exhortation by Moses as a sacred command.[32]

Hear, O Israel: The LORD our God, the LORD is one. Love the LORD your God with all your heart and with all your soul and with all your strength. These commandments that I give you today are to be on your hearts.

— Deuteronomy 6:4–6 (NIV)

The Hebrew people believed that the heart was the most inward part of man. Before a heart can be filled with love for God and the love of God, it must be redeemed and reformed. Through our confession and conversion, God removes our "stony heart" (Ezekiel 11:19). He replaces it with a heart that is "clean" (Psalm 51:10), and one's heart must learn to be "fixed on Him" (Psalm 112:7); as well as consumed with respect and reverence for the Lord (verse 1). It is "with your heart that you believe and are justified" (Romans 10:10, NIV), and in the "heart," the power of God is exercised for the purpose of renewing us daily (Jeremiah 31:33).[33]

The reconstruction of our hearts is for the purpose of us being filled with God's love and is vital to prophetic ministry, but especially for those who seek to live the treasured values of heaven. In fact, between Paul's exhortations concerning the manifestation and correct demonstration of the spiritual gifts of the Spirit in 1 Corinthians 12 and 14, Paul exhorts us to love. For the basis of true ministry is love.

We see this in the ministry of the Lord Jesus, His disciples, Paul, and those Paul mentored. Love is fundamental to both God and man. A heart full of love must be the prerequisite in everything we are and do. The Lord Jesus made known to those closest to Him that the teachings found in both the law and prophets had to be received in love (Matthew 22:40; Mark 12:28–34). Then

A heart full of love must be the prerequisite in everything we are and do.

the apostle Paul, in 1 Corinthians 13, declared that love is the greatest of all the graces of our life in Christ. Yes, even to those who were tremendously used prophetically in the Corinthian church, Paul said that love is greater than speaking with tongues, the gift of prophecy, or the possession of supernatural and extraordinary faith. In verse eight of chapter thirteen, Paul writes, "Love never fails. But where there are prophecies, they will cease; where there are tongues, they will be stilled; where there is knowledge, it will pass away" (NIV). He fully understood that without love, all these great spiritual gifts and graces, desirable and useful as they are in themselves, are basically nothing without love and ultimately have little, if any, permanent value in the sight of God.[34]

But where does such love begin? It begins with God. In 1 John 4:7–8 (NIV) (emphasis added by the author), the apostle wrote,

Dear friends, let us love one another, for love comes from God. Everyone who loves has been born of God and knows God. Whoever does not love does not know God, because God is love.

And in 1 John 4:16–19 (NIV),

And so we know and rely on the love God has for us. God is love. Whoever lives in love lives in God, and God in them. This is how love is made complete among us so that we will have confidence on the day of judgment: In this world we are like Jesus. There is no fear in love. But perfect love drives out fear, because fear has to do with punishment. The one who fears is not made perfect in love. We love because he first loved us.

God loves us because He is love. Love is not something He does but who He is. One cannot separate God from His love. His love is complete, constant, and consistent. It is through love that He beckons us from the darkness to come into His marvelous light. Without threat or harm, He calls out to us because He is love. And, when we open our hearts to Him, Paul said, "The love of God is shed abroad in our hearts by the Holy Ghost which is given unto us" (Romans 5:5, KJV). Whoever lives in love lives in God, and God in him. One awesome aspect of God's love is that it drives out all fear. And, by becoming fully aware that God's Divine Spirit lives and dwells within your heart, you will know that He desires for His love to be forming, lifting, enlightening, guiding, constraining, and filling your life with more and more of His love.[35]

From the moment we believe in the Lord Jesus Christ, the Holy Spirit and the love of God take up residence in our hearts. But, as His temple on the earth, we are the ones who choose how much of the house we are going to let Him live in. It appears that there are some believers that only allow His love to abide in their "living room or the public places of their life." These folks struggle to allow Him and His love into other parts of their lives. Still, others allow Him to fill the "bedrooms" of their life and open themselves to His loving intimacy but refuse to allow Him into certain closets, where their "secret lives" are stored. It has been my experience that the Holy Spirit will never force His way into the different parts of our hearts. Yes, He will coax, encourage, and persuade. But it is up to us to open the doors of every part of our hearts. And by opening our hearts all the way, He will come in, commune with us, filling our lives with His love all the way to the brim and running over into the lives of everyone we meet.

Embracing the development of prophetic ministry and the coming move of God must be founded in love. God's light, life, and love are the foundation for all the other treasures in heaven. Because His love never fails, the foundation of His love will not fail. By fully opening ourselves to the Spirit of wisdom and revelation (Ephesians 1:17), we come to know, like prophecy, God's love cannot be fully explained, only experienced. God's love calls to be fully experienced for,

> *Love is patient, love is kind. It does not envy, it does not boast, it is not proud. It does not dishonor others, it is not self-seeking, it is not easily angered, it keeps no record of wrongs. Love does not delight in evil but rejoices with the truth. It always protects, always trusts, always hopes, always perseveres.*
>
> — 1 Corinthians 13:4–7 (NIV)

As our heart finds delight in Him, possessing and sharing His love becomes the desire of our heart. He promises to fulfill the desires of those who delight in Him (Psalm 37:4). Paul told Timothy that love pours from a pure heart, a good conscience, and a sincere faith. These are what some have called the three conditions of spiritual growth, but it all begins with love.

It is the apostle John who speaks to the wondrous depth and transforming power of God's love. First, as a disciple, John was one of the two sons of Zebedee (Matthew 4:21). Jesus gave John and his brother James the Hebrew nickname *Boanerges*, which literally means *sons of thunder.*[36] This nickname may have been given to the brothers because they were known for their fiery temperament (Luke 9:34) or their unwavering commitment to follow Jesus no matter the cost. Much is to be learned about the apostle John's heart from his writing. Not only was John a disciple and apostle of Jesus, but he forsook everything to follow Jesus and was the only one that followed Christ all the way to the cross (John 19:26). His gospel (quite different in structure than the other three) is nothing short of being his own spiritual biography, which describes his own personal growth, especially in the areas of faith and love.

John was part of the Lord's inner circle (along with James and Peter). Over time, he apparently became the nearest to Jesus and even described himself as "the disciple whom Jesus loved" (John 13:23; 20:2; 21:7, 20). Due to his deep heart experience of the Lord's love, and because of that love, John became the apostle who wrote most about the love of God. His intensity toward the subject of love reveals not only his total commitment and devotion toward Christ but it shows in the intensity of his distaste and disgust toward sin and anything "anti-Christ."

John became the apostle who wrote most about the love of God.

In the book of Revelation (the last book of the New Testament), John was given both exciting and powerful prophetic visions while being *in the Spirit on the Lord's day* (Revelation 1:10; 4:1–2). The theme of the prophecy concerns the conflict of Christ and His church with anti-Christian powers (the devil, the beast, the false prophet; see Revelation 16:13) and the ultimate and decisive defeat of the latter.[37] But most of all, the prophecy reveals John's abiding and undying love for his Lord and master, Jesus Christ. Throughout John's life, his initial love for Christ never waned but rather grew deeper, wider, broader, and higher each and every day. John's heart was fully toward the Lord and overflowed with the love of God toward the Lord and others.

> *This is how God showed his love among us: He sent his one and only Son into the world that we might live through him. This is love: not that we loved God, but that he loved us and sent his Son as an atoning sacrifice for our sins. Dear friends, since God so loved us, we also ought to love one another.*
>
> — 1 John 4:9–11 (NIV)

CHAPTER NINE:

Thinking with a Righteous Mind

For, "who has known the mind of the Lord so as to instruct him?" But we have the mind of Christ.

— 1 Corinthians 2:16 (NIV)

The mind of the *pneumatikos*, i.e., *spiritual* or *prophetic man*, in Paul's letter to the Corinthians, is depicted as both exceptional and spiritually developed in contrast to those who only desire to know Christ in a carnal and immature way. The mysteries of God being revealed to us are in direct proportion to our having a heart filled with the love of God and an openness to becoming spiritually minded. In his epistle to the Romans, the apostle Paul wrote,

The mind governed by the flesh is death, but the mind governed by the Spirit is life and peace. The mind governed by the flesh is hostile to God; it does not submit to God's law, nor can it do so.

— Romans 8:6–7 (NIV)

To Paul, the mind included all the faculties of perceiving and understanding both the natural and supernatural world. The saved mind (in contrast to the sinful mind) possesses the capacity for spiritual (in contrast to religious) truth. *To have the mind of Christ* means that one has sought after and then, with the help of the Holy Spirit, developed the ability to perceive divine things, such as recognizing God's blessing as well as learning to fully hate evil. Such a spiritual-minded person can consider and judge thoughtfully, insightfully, and impartially. The Pauline definition no doubt included his understanding of the Greek *ginosko*, which means to learn to know, come to know, perceive, and understand. It is related to a Jewish idiom that spoke to the sexual intercourse between a man and a woman. *Ginosko* describes more than intellectual knowledge but experiential knowledge, understanding, and wisdom.[38]

A spiritual-minded person can consider and judge thoughtfully, insightfully, and impartially.

Paul's exhortation in 1 Corinthians 2: 7–16 is called a *midrash* or *rabbinic interpretation* of Scripture (see Isaiah 64:4). Here, Paul speaks to his revelation and the spiritual truth that the sinful and carnal mind of a person cannot understand the things of God and, therefore, is blind to the light of the gospel and the mysteries of God. In his second letter to the Corinthians, Paul wrote these words, "The god of this age has blinded the minds of unbelievers, so that they cannot see the light of the gospel that displays the glory of Christ, who is the image of God" (2 Corinthians 4:4, NIV). Without the love of Christ dwelling in our heart, our mind is unable to perceive the smallest of spiritual things.

It also follows that to the degree which we open ourselves and are filled with the love of God will ultimately determine the level of our ability to have the mind of Christ and to perceive the things of God.

Paul spoke about this in Romans 12:1–2 (NIV),

> *Therefore, I urge you, brothers and sisters, in view of God's mercy, to offer your bodies as a living sacrifice, holy and pleasing to God—this is your true and proper worship. Do not conform to the pattern of this world, but be transformed by the renewing of your mind. Then you will be able to test and approve what God's will is—his good, pleasing and perfect will.*

Refusing to conform to our old pattern of thinking (the world's thinking) and rejecting the way we used to look at things (the world's view of things) is only part of the solution. We must be willing and seek to offer ourselves as living sacrifices so that we will be transformed (present passive imperative of *metamorphoô*) by the spiritual renewing of our mind. This radical change in the inner man happens within the new heart and a renewed and transformed mind. It continues as we are willing to experience *ongoing spiritual metamorphosis* or *shift*.

I love what Dr. Patrick Oben said about the concept of ongoing spiritual metamorphosis. He said,

> *God's design is to be transformed into the fullness of the image of Christ in us. When we are born again, the seed of God is planted within us, and our spirit [heart] is recreated as the new man. God wants our outward, visible life (especially our outward manner of*

life) to undergo a complete makeover. This implies our outward form or behavior is powered by our mindset. Whatever changes our mind, will also change our life. As we meditate on the Word of God, our old way of thinking is gradually replaced by God's Word [the way He thinks]. As this change occurs, our outward life will change from a spiritual egg to a caterpillar, pupa and then a beautiful butterfly.[39]

The transformation of our mind enables us to enter a new mode of existence in Christ Jesus. As we begin to conform our thinking to the Word of God, heavenly principles start taking shape in our lives. We not only begin to love as Jesus loves but think as He thinks. Such transformation is nothing short of spiritual revolution. And our example is Jesus, the Word (Logos). "And the Word, entering a new mode of existence, became flesh, and lived in a tent [His physical body] among us" (John 1:14, Wuest New Testament).

The *Logos*, prior to His earthly birth, existed as God and with God from eternity. But the *Logos became…the Son!*

> *In the beginning was the Word, and the Word was with God, and the Word was God. He was with God in the beginning. … The Word became flesh and made his dwelling among us. We have seen his glory, the glory of the one and only Son, who came from the Father, full of grace and truth.*
>
> — John 1:1–2, 14 (NIV)

Hebrews 1:5 (NIV) says, "For to which of the angels did God ever say, 'You are my Son; today I have become your Father'?"

Through the incarnation of Jesus (the Word), He moved from life as the Word to life as the only begotten Son. The eternal Word had never been a Son in the flesh—until He was born of the virgin Mary and became the begotten Son in the flesh. And that Son is the only begotten of the Father, Jesus Christ. The Word was only Spirit until He (the Lord Jesus) became a man in the flesh. By doing so, He gave us the opportunity to be like Him. "This is how love is made complete among us so that we will have confidence on the day of judgment: In this world *we are like Jesus*" (1 John 4:17, NIV) (emphasis added by the author).

What are the sacrifices, sufferings, and rewards of our entering into this new mode of existence? The process of our entering the new mode called *sonship requires us to die to self and to surrender our way of thinking about our* personal will, agenda, and rights. It means to give up our minds for His. Paul explains it like this,

> *Have the same mindset as Christ Jesus: Who, being in very nature God, did not consider equality with God something to be used to his own advantage; rather, he made himself nothing by taking the very nature of a servant, being made in human likeness. And being found in appearance as a man, he humbled himself by becoming obedient to death—even death on a cross!*
>
> — Philippians 2:5–8 (NIV)

Christ, the Word (Spirit without the limitation of time or space), became flesh (in a body limited by both time and space).

This was done so Adam's original sin could be dealt with, our salvation be paid for, and we might be filled with the treasures of heaven.

> *But we have this treasure in jars of clay to show that*
> *this all-surpassing power is from God and not from us.*
>
> — 2 Corinthians 4:7 (NIV)

This treasure is more than having a *ticket to heaven*. It is Christ in us, the hope of glory! It is the illuminating power of the glory of God (verse 6). "The power is limitless, but it is stored in very unlikely receptacles" (Plummer). And now His power has now taken up residence in but earthen (Greek: *ostracon*) or baked clay vessels. We have been chosen as earthen jars to be used by God for His purposes (Romans 9:20), even though we are so fragile in comparison to Him. God's purpose is to reveal "the preeminence of His power and greatness through us." God, not man, is the dynamo (*dunamis*) or power behind this. The power that is transforming our lives comes from God (*tou theou*) and does not originate with us.[40]

We have been chosen as earthen jars to be used by God for His purposes.

The reward of being filled with God's treasure must be seen as not just for our benefit but for the sake of others. Heaven's rewards include our ability to receive revelation and to be entrusted with the secret things of God. When asked who His disciples believed Him to be;

> *Simon Peter answered, "You are the Messiah, the Son*
> *of the living God." Jesus replied, "Blessed are you,*

Simon son of Jonah, for this was not revealed to you by flesh and blood, but by my Father in heaven."

— Matthew 16:16–17 (NIV)

The apostle Paul gives us a similar understanding in 1 Corinthians 2:9–10 (NIV),

However, as it is written: "What no eye has seen, what no ear has heard, and what no human mind has conceived"—the things God has prepared for those who love him— these are the things God has revealed to us by his Spirit.

This, then, is how you ought to regard us: as servants of Christ and as those entrusted with the mysteries God has revealed. Now it is required that those who have been given a trust must prove faithful.

—1 Corinthians 4:1 (NIV)

To fully embrace the coming prophetic movement, we must be renewed in the spirit of our mind; and put on the new man, through the working of the Holy Spirit, is created in righteousness and true holiness (Ephesians 4:23–24). This "brand-new man" must follow and live after the pattern Son (Jesus Christ) and seek to be like Him in all things (including the way we think—see Romans 8:29)

We must also commit to having incorporated into our lives the "message of reconciliation."

All this is from God, who reconciled us to himself
through Christ and gave us the ministry of reconcili-
ation: that God was reconciling the world to himself
in Christ, not counting people's sins against them. And
he has committed to us the message of reconciliation.
We are therefore Christ's ambassadors, as though God
were making his appeal through us. We implore you
on Christ's behalf: Be reconciled to God. God made
him who had no sin to be sin for us, so that in him we
might become the righteousness of God.

— 2 Corinthians 5:18–21 (NIV)

I believe that in that meeting before time began, the Father, the Son, and the Holy Spirit were there, and this question was considered and answered by the eternal heart and mind of God, "What price is too high to pay to display the hope of glory in the lives of men?" And if God invited you to a meeting with Him today, I believe He would ask you the question, "What price would be too high to pay for us to have His glory displayed in your life?" In John 17:4 (NIV), Jesus said to the Father, "I have brought you glory on earth by finishing the work you gave me to do." "And the glory which You gave Me I have given them, that they may be one just as We are one" (John 17:22, NKJV). Jesus paid the ultimate price. He came to this world, fully God and fully man. He became obedient unto death, even death on the cross. Now He is seated at the right hand of God in heaven. We should think constantly of Him and as He would have us think.

Will you embrace your new heart and mind? Will you be conformed to His Word and transformed in your mind by the Holy Spirit? Will you allow the Holy Spirit to replace the sinful corruption of the past with His glory and righteousness? Will you open your thinking to the coming fresh outpouring of the Holy Spirit? If you will, the impossible will be possible. For nothing is impossible with God!

CHAPTER TEN:

The Attitude of Gratitude

Therefore, since we are receiving a kingdom that cannot be shaken, let us be thankful, and so worship God acceptably with reverence and awe.

— Hebrews 12:28 (NIV)

So far in our process, we have examined the foundational spiritual truths that are necessary to make it possible for us to encounter and embrace the coming prophetic outpouring. We have sought to bring illumination concerning the spiritual development of both the heart and mind. I now would like to address the second part of the process, which is needed for us to move from concept to precept. A concept is the apprehension of an idea. It can be either a spiritual or mental act by which a person sees or shapes intent. A precept, on the other hand, is an action that is based on concept. It is any commandment or order intended as an authoritative rule of action but applied particularly to commands respecting moral conduct.[41]

The Holy Spirit continually seeks to develop in us a fully regenerated heart and a transformed mind in order that we would be able to consider all the possibilities found in Christ.

Such possibilities are founded on a love that is both vast and infinite. When we think of the love of Jesus being manifested in and through us, how He paid the ultimate price that we might become heirs and joint heirs with Him, and that, as God's sons and daughters, we have been enabled to live in a new and living way, our attitude should be overflowing with gratitude. Why? Because a grateful attitude is the outward expression of both godly and righteous emotion.

It is also the attitude that those with spiritual understanding see as necessary for the transformation of their mind to continue. I have found that one who does not possess a heart full of love and a changed mind will likely sense no real need to have or show gratitude. Such people seem to lack the desire to give thanks and glorify God, not just for all the gifts He has given them, but because He is the giver of everything that pertains to all life and godliness.

Without gratitude, people become comfortable and spiritually stuck. Gratitude causes us to know that everything we have and are is from Him. It also helps us see that God is greater than anything we face in life. Pastor Tony Evans said,

> *God says to give thanks in everything. That doesn't mean you need to give thanks for everything. You don't need to give thanks for that bad day. Or for that bad relationship. Or being passed over at work. Financial hardship. Whatever it is – you are not to give thanks for the difficulties, but rather in the difficulties. That is a very important distinction, and one I think we often miss. Giving thanks in everything shows a heart of faith that God is bigger than the difficulties and that*

He can use them, if you approach Him with the right heart and spirit, for your good and His glory.

Giving thanks with a grateful heart opens the heart's spiritual eyes. Gratitude enables one to have a better sense of God's Presence and reminds us that God is for us; therefore, nothing can stand against us. In fact, gratitude pulls us toward Him, deepens our faith, and opens the door to His unspeakable joy. Gratitude is the attitude that must fill our life. Why? The precept of giving thanks, or of being grateful, reminds us how much God values us, which means that we have value beyond what we have or think. If we are only focused on the things we want God to bless us with, we lose the wonder of the benefits He has already given to us. Such also causes us to focus on what we want rather than on the treasures that we already possess.

Gratitude enables one to have a better sense of God's Presence.

In his letter to the Colossians, the apostle Paul encouraged the correct response to the blessing of God upon their lives, "Let the message of Christ dwell among you richly as you teach and admonish one another with all wisdom through psalms, hymns, and songs from the Spirit, singing to God with gratitude in your hearts" (Colossians 3:16, NIV).

With the same frame of mind, King David put it this way,

Enter his gates with thanksgiving and his courts with praise; give thanks to him and praise his name. For the LORD is good and his love endures forever; his faithfulness continues through all generations.

— Psalm 100:4–5 (NIV)

Gratitude was David's go-to response to the blessing of God. Let us join him in remembering all the things the Lord has done for us. Let us give thanks for all the benefits (treasures) which have already been deposited into our lives by Lord. In Psalm 103, David said we should,

> *Praise the LORD, my soul, and forget not all his benefits—who forgives all your sins and heals all your diseases, who redeems your life from the pit and crowns you with love and compassion, who satisfies your desires with good things so that your youth is renewed like the eagle's.*
>
> — Psalm 103:2–5 (NIV)

What a list! From this short list, our gratefulness should be reaching heaven's throne room! Like David, I encourage you to start your own record of the good things the Lord has put within your life. Consider that His goodness kept you before you came to Christ, and His goodness continues to keep you in His loving kindness and mercy. The Lord does not return evil for evil but seeks to show His mercy and grace toward us all. He does treat us as *damaged goods* but as saints of the Highest God; He sees us not as servants or slaves but dearly loved sons and daughters. He freely gives us His inheritance instead of wages and blessing instead of punishment. The goodness of God's love should be greatly recognized and cause Him to be highly exalted by our hearts, minds, and voices. His loving delight for us is shown by His glorious benevolence, which explains His disdain for those who exhibit injustice and meanness toward us.

How long can we count on His love? Forever! And ever and ever! This is due to His great faithfulness, which He executes presently and will continue to pour out upon generation after generation. And if we go no further on our list, what should our response be? What level of gratefulness is appropriate for all the great things He has done?

I become amused when watching the fans who attend a sporting event. The team on the field or court is doing nothing directly with the fans, but the fans act like every touchdown, goal, or home run is being accomplished by them and for them! Whether the fans are in Seattle, Kansas City, or London, every time there is a goal or their team dunks a basketball or scores the winning touchdown, the fans begin shouting…whistling…clapping! Many begin jumping up and down! Some fans even begin dancing. Sadly, some of those same people think to offer such a demonstration over the goodness of the Lord is a little overboard. Gratefulness does not always have to be shared with exuberance, but it doesn't hurt. The reason is simple, an attitude of gratitude is the difference between those who thrive and those who survive.

King David was a *thriver!* His positive attitude about God and the people of God made a huge difference in his approach to life. His life and reign stood in stark contrast to his predecessor, King Saul. There is a story that illustrates how David felt about his God and the opportunity that had been given to him. In 2 Samuel 6:1–14, we read about King David bringing the ark of the covenant into Jerusalem. During his first attempt, David had not followed the prescribed way the ark should be carried. Sadly, David's mistake cost Uzzah his life. But David learned from his mistake and several months later called upon the priests to carry the ark into Jerusalem upon their shoulders. In verse fourteen of

2 Samuel 6, we read that as the ark was being brought into the city, "David danced before the Lord with all his might." In other words, he held nothing back. David poured out all the musical and lyrical emotion he had in his devout soul. The Bible references that there was at least one person (his wife) who did not appreciate his exuberance. I believe David had a deep spiritual understanding of the power that would flow from his grateful attitude that day. Hebrews 4:7 attributes the following happy and enthusiastic *royal psalm* to King David.

> *Come, let us sing for joy to the LORD; let us shout aloud to the Rock of our salvation. Let us come before him with thanksgiving and extol him with music and song. For the LORD is the great God, the great King above all gods. In his hand are the depths of the earth, and the mountain peaks belong to him. The sea is his, for he made it, and his hands formed the dry land. Come, let us bow down in worship, let us kneel before the LORD our Maker, for he is our God and we are the people of his pasture, the flock under his care.*
>
> — Psalm 95:1–7 (NIV)

David's attitude of gratitude speaks to his awesome relationship with God, His maker. David was enlightened and given spiritual understanding while giving praise to God. But it wasn't only David who experienced God's enlightenment. Elisha was called upon to prophesy the Word of the Lord in 2 Kings 3:15–16 (KJV). But before Elisha would speak, he said, "But now bring me a minstrel. And it came to pass, when the minstrel played, that the hand of the LORD came upon him. And he said, Thus saith the LORD."

An attitude of gratefulness also brings great contentment. I love what Pastor Max Lucado said about gratitude and contentment. He said,

> *Gratitude is a mindful awareness of the benefits of life. It is the greatest of virtues. Gratitude leads us off the riverbank of "if only" and escorts us into the fertile valley of "already." The anxious heart says, "Lord, if only I had this, that, or the other, I'd be ok." The grateful heart says, "Oh, look! You've already given me this, that, and the other. Thank you, God.*[42]

Contented people find it easy to keep their thoughts off their troubles and focus on the wonderful provision God has provided and will provide in their lives. They look forward rather than backward in life. Studies have linked the emotion of gratitude with a variety of positive effects. Grateful people tend to be more empathetic and forgiving of others. People who keep a gratitude journal are more likely to have a positive outlook on life. Grateful individuals demonstrate less envy, materialism, and self-comparison. Thankfulness improves self-esteem and enhances relationships, quality of sleep, and longevity.[43]

Grateful individuals demonstrate less envy, materialism, and self-comparison.

Paul revealed this level of contentment when he was being held in prison in Rome. Writing to the Philippians, Paul shared with them that while he was very grateful for their prayers and concern about his situation,

God had revealed to him that the situation had changed. It had become clear to him that he was not actually chained to the prison guard, but the prison guard had been chained to him! The Lord had used Paul's proximity to the palace guards to give him an opportunity to testify to them about Christ. He told the church that many of the palace guards had come to Christ, and many of the nearby brothers in the Lord were being encouraged to speak the word with boldness. Paul's attitude of gratefulness enabled him to minister more courageously and fearlessly (see Philippians 1:12–14).

We must never forget that our circumstances are never the end of the story. The Lord is using everything for our good and the good of those who are watching Him work in our lives. One of the most powerful testimonies we can offer is that we are truly grateful despite our circumstances. We must always remember the exhortation of Romans 8:37 (NIV), "No, in all these things we are more than conquerors through him who loved us." We not only overcome all sufferings and tragedy but are also more than conquerors in all of them.

"Therefore by Him let us continually offer the sacrifice of praise to God, that is, the fruit of our lips, giving thanks to His name" (Hebrews 13:15, NKJV).

CHAPTER ELEVEN:

The Reward of Faith

And without faith it is impossible to please God,
because anyone who comes to him must believe *that*
he exists and that he rewards *those who earnestly seek*
him.

— Hebrews 11:6 (NIV)
(emphasis added by the author)

The next precept we will consider is the reward of faith. Faith is being sure of what we hope for and certain of what we do not see (Hebrews 11:1). For one to be in possession of faith, one must be fully persuaded, to the point of certainty, as to a person or object. When we reach that degree of being convinced, complete trust and full confidence in God occurs. Theologically speaking, a person who possesses faith expresses their belief in the truth of the gospel by fully yielding their heart (will) and mind (intellect) to God. The work of salvation is a result of a person's trust in and reliance upon Christ. Faith in God is a choice. Faith rests on our choice to believe the divine revelation illuminated to us by the Word of God and the Holy Spirit (Matthew 16:17).

Faith has both rewards and positive consequences. In other words, faith is the firm belief in the genuineness of God's testimony and confidence in the certainty of those things which God has declared because He is the one who has declared them. What are the rewards of such faith?

There is a dramatic effect on the life of anyone who makes the decision to believe in God and His Word. Just as gratitude makes an impact on our attitude, faith brings about both temporal and eternal rewards. God has promised to reward those who are diligent in their belief. The apostle Paul wrote,

God has promised to reward those who are diligent in their belief.

> *Whatever you do, work at it with all your heart, as working for the Lord, not for human masters, since you know that you will receive an inheritance from the Lord as a reward. It is the Lord Christ you are serving.*
>
> — Colossians 3:23–24 (NIV)

The Greek phrase Paul used to describe the *reward of inheritance* in verse twenty-four is *misthos kleronomia*. Paul used the phrase to describe the fruit that naturally results from work or investment. It speaks to the repayment of both the temporal and the eternal bestowed blessing that results from faith.[44] One cannot sow the seed of faith without receiving the reward of God's blessing (Matthew 13:31–32). God is the rewarder (*ho misthapodotês*) or the one who *gives to or rewards those who diligently seek Him* in Hebrews 11:6. The Hebrews writer wanted his readers to understand that there is always a future reward bestowed by God. The reward begins with a relationship with God Himself. Like Enoch, who was rewarded for "walking with God" (Genesis 5:24). His reward? God took him. Those who walk with God by faith will be taken by Him into immeasurable reams of glory! Jesus also said that those who are insulted and persecuted because of their faith in Him will receive that same promise.

> *Blessed are you when people insult you, persecute you and falsely say all kinds of evil against you because of me. Rejoice and be glad, because great is your reward in heaven, for in the same way they persecuted the prophets who were before you.*
>
> — Matthew 5:11–12 (NIV)

Paul wrote to the Corinthian church in 1 Corinthians 3:6–9 (NIV) that along with our faith, our spiritual labor will also be rewarded.

> *I planted the seed, Apollos watered it, but God has been making it grow. So neither the one who plants nor the one who waters is anything, but only God, who makes things grow. The one who plants and the one who waters have one purpose, and they will each be rewarded according to their own labor. For we are co-workers in God's service; you are God's field, God's building.*

It is important to note that it is not only the works we do that are rewarded but the faith in God that enables us to produce those good works. Such faith (Greek: *pistis*) is the heartfelt conviction that God exists and is the creator and ruler of all things. He is the provider and bestower of eternal salvation through Jesus Christ. And by putting our trust in Him, we become sons and daughters of God, heirs of the kingdom of God and His righteousness.[45] Faith then enables us to receive what He has promised (Hebrews 10:36).

One of the early church declarations concerning belief, faith, and the rewards of such is found in what later became known as the Apostles' Creed, sometimes called the "Old Roman Creed." The origin of this *creed* is not clear, but its early form is likely preserved in the *Interrogatory Creed of Hippolytus' Apostolic Tradition*. The earliest written form of this creed is found in a letter that Marcellus of Ancyra wrote in Greek to Julius, the bishop of Rome, about AD 341. About fifty years later, Tyrannius Rufinus wrote *Commentarius in Symbolum Apostolorum*. In it, he recounted the viewpoint that the apostles wrote the creed together after Pentecost before leaving Jerusalem to preach. The title "Apostles' Creed" is also mentioned in AD 390 by Ambrose. The text of the Old Roman Creed is as follows, with the last phrase (included by Marcellus but omitted by Rufinus) in parentheses.[46]

I believe in God the Father Almighty; and in Christ Jesus His only Son, our Lord, Who was born from the Holy Spirit and the Virgin Mary, Who under Pontius Pilate was crucified and buried, on the third day rose again from the dead, ascended into heaven, sits at the right hand of the Father, whence he will come to judge the living and the dead; and in the Holy Spirit, the holy Church, [now get ready...here comes the reward]... the remission of sins, the resurrection of the flesh, (and life everlasting).[47]

The rewards of faith in God are endless. I do not have the time or the space to begin to mention them all because they are too numerous for us to comprehend without them being revealed to us by the Spirit (1 Corinthians 2:10). But I do want to hopefully inspire you toward believing for a great and wonderful spiritual restoration and reformation by offering a few of them.

The first reward I want to share has to do with sin. This modern age has gone so soft on sin that most sins are not seen as sins. Sin has become an illness to be either medically or psychologically dealt with rather than a condition that needs to be redeemed from. But the Word of God continues to be true. Sin separates man from God, and the wages of sin is death (Romans 6:23). No amount of medicine or therapy can remove sin. Only faith in Jesus Christ will bring about the reward of redemption and reconciliation. Through our trust in His death, burial, and resurrection, the penalty of sin (death) is removed, and grace then destroys the power (authority) that sin has over us and replaces the presence of sin with righteousness (heart), peace (mind), and joy (attitude) in the Holy Spirit (see Romans 14:17). Faith in God does not simply provide forgiveness of the sins we have committed. Faith in God provides the only remedy for the effect of Adam's original rebellion against God and gives us the ability to overcome even the temptation of sin!

> *There hath no temptation taken you but such as*
> *is common to man: but God is faithful, who will*
> *not suffer you to be tempted above that ye are able*
> *[reward!]; but will with the temptation also make a*

way to escape [reward!], that ye may be able to bear it [reward!].

— 1 Corinthians 10:13

The second reward is found in our everyday walk with the Lord. God's faithfulness is one of the marvelous characteristics of His nature and an awesome reward. Our relationship with and in Him rewards us with His trustworthiness, His consistency, and His faithfulness. Because He is constant and faithful in keeping His promises, He is fully worthy of all our trust, as illustrated in the following story.

Once in a Charles S. Price revival meeting, a little seven-year-old girl came to the platform. Dr. Price asked her, "Tell me, dear, what is your trouble?" Her answer was a very pained expression on her face. She slowly lifted her limb and revealed to Dr. Price a very badly crippled and deformed little foot. Her foot was encased in a special large and extremely bulky shoe. Price then noticed that under her arm, the girl was holding something that she seemed to value. "What have you in the parcel, little girl?" he asked. Slowly, in full view of the audience, she unfastened the string and unrolled the paper, and to his astonished eyes, she presented a new shoe. She held it up very proudly and then prophetically exclaimed, "I brought it with me so I could wear it home." (Now, that is faith in God!)

That evening the unspoiled and untarnished faith of that little child reached out and stood upon the promises of God with simple childlike faith. Dr. Price anointed her forehead with oil and prayed, "My little sister, receive your healing in the Name of Jesus." Many said there was no expression of ecstatic joy that left her lips. She offered no outburst of emotionalism. She simply took her new shoe and very deliberately walked over to a nearby chair and began to unfasten the old shoe on her crippled foot and put the new shoe on. Then something wonderful happened! The reward of her faith. The reward of her prophetic utterance! The Lord healed her foot! They who witnessed the event stood in amazement. She simply walked off the stage wearing her new shoe on the foot that had been crippled. Someone asked, "Who healed you, dear?" To which she replied, "Jesus." Then she said, "Somebody throw that old shoe away; I won't need it anymore!" Hallelujah! A little child taught a great audience that night the difference between passive faith and the kind of active faith that receives the reward.

It is that kind of faith that Abraham came to know and live by. Abraham experienced God's glorious provision and unchangeableness. He was willing to trade all that he had for a promise. He believed in God's spoken word to him as well as God's steadfastness and fidelity. We see this in His initial covenant promise to Abraham (that has been handed from generation to generation). Genesis 15:1 (NIV) says, "After this, the word of the LORD came to Abram in a vision: 'Do not be afraid, Abram. I am your shield, your very great reward.'"

Abraham was willing to trade all that he had for a promise.

Consider Abraham; he "believed God, and it was credited to him as righteousness" (Romans 4:3, NIV). Abraham believed God was a rewarder to those that put their trust in Him. And Abraham was right! He believed in God and was rewarded with his son of promise, Isaac. He believed in God and was rewarded with the provision of a sacrificial ram that brought rescue to his son of promise. He believed in God again and was rewarded in that his servant found the exact woman God had prepared for his son. His faith blessed not only him, his family, and his nation but all humanity. That includes us! And speaking of Abraham,

> *By faith he made his home in the promised land like a stranger in a foreign country; he lived in tents, as did Isaac and Jacob, who were heirs with him of the same promise. [And now by faith—so are we!] For he was looking forward to the city with foundations, whose architect and builder is God.*
>
> — Hebrews 11:9–10 (NIV)

The third reward can be found in the glorious riches of God's grace. The bestowal of this reward is given so that we might be strengthened in our inmost being. Recorded in Ephesians for the sake of all believers, Paul prayed that the eyes of our hearts might be enlightened in order that we may know the hope to which He has called us, the riches of his glorious inheritance in the saints, and his incomparably great power for us who believe (Ephesians 1:18–19).

The result of such faith? That we can grasp the hugeness of what God desires to do in the days ahead! I am convinced that, like in the days of Elijah the prophet, there is a new outpouring of the Spirit on the horizon (1 Kings 18:44). I hear the sound of a deluge of the Spirit coming toward us. The hand of the Lord will be put afresh and anew on those who believe and seek His face! (See 1 Kings 18:4–46.) He will reward our faith as He did Noah, Abraham, Moses, David, and all the others listed in Hebrews 11. Step up to the plate! Gird up your loins! And as Bishop T. D. Jakes says, "Get ready! Get ready! Get ready!"

CHAPTER TWELVE:

Balancing Humility and Confidence

The fruit of that righteousness will be peace; its effect will be quietness and confidence forever.

— Isaiah 32:17 (NIV)

A heart full of righteousness will always produce peace of mind. The effect of that righteousness and peace will be a calm, quiet humility and confidence placed in God's faithfulness, power, and love. As we prepare for the next awesome outpouring of the Spirit, I want to offer the example of our Lord and Savior, Jesus Christ. He experienced the Holy Spirit coming upon Him at His baptism. He testified to the result of such several days later in a synagogue in Capernaum (Luke 4:17–21). For almost three years, He healed the sick, cast out demons, fed the multitude, and preached the kingdom of God. (See Matthew 4:17; Luke 4:38–41; John 6:1–14.)

Throughout His ministry, He showed an amazing balance of humility and confidence. In Matthew 17:1–5, we read the account of the transfiguration of Jesus. Along with His three closest disciples (Peter, James, and John), there were two other attendees. Their names were Moses and Elijah. According to Exodus, Moses had died and been buried around 1400 years before by the Lord, Himself (Deuteronomy 34:6). And Elijah had escaped death by leaving the planet in a chariot of fire and horses (2 Kings 2:11). Matthew records that both great Old Testament men of God arrived on the Mount of Transfiguration supernaturally and without warning. They stood alongside Jesus, Moses on one side and Elijah on the other. Almost immediately, a cloud of heaven's shekinah glory enshrouded the top of the mountain hiding heaven's glorious light that burst forth and transfigured the Lord's body from the inside out.

On one side of the Son of God stood Moses. He was known to have meekness above all the men which were upon the face of the earth (Numbers 12:2), and this notwithstanding the tremendous divine revelation given him on Mount Sinai (Exodus 34:29–30). Moses' revelation of the glory of God transcends the speculations of theologians about God. While most speculations are cold and lifeless, the revelation given to Moses was alive, powerful, and glorious. The things Moses experienced exceed the capacity of the human intellect. The descriptive and indicative words used by Moses throughout the Torah give exaltation and glory to Him who is beyond the natural man's expression and comprehension.

On the other hand, stood the great prophet and firebrand Elijah. Having gained the reputation as the most zealous defender of the Holy One of Israel (See 1 Kings 18), Elijah had left the planet into the glories of immortality by riding a chariot of fire in a whirlwind (2 Kings 2:11).

Why were they there? I believe that, yes, they were representatives of the law and the prophets. But, more than that, they were there to speak to the new dimension that was about to take place in the realm of the Spirit. Perhaps because they both understood the concept of departing from one realm into another. They had lived lives filled with the manifestation of God's glory and witnessed their own "exodus."

The purpose of the transfiguration was for Jesus to be encouraged by His heavenly Father concerning His approaching death and to give His three chosen disciples a glimpse of His coming victory over death, hell, and the grave. Apparently, there wasn't one of them who fully understood the passion or purpose of Jesus. So, Moses and Elijah were sent from heaven. Along with them, heaven's glorious light literally overwhelmed Peter, James, and John.

> *The purpose of the transfiguration was to strengthen the firm resolve of Jesus.*

Moses and Elijah then began talking with Jesus about the very subject concerning which Peter had dared to rebuke Jesus for mentioning in Matthew 16:22. As the *shekinah cloud* of God's glory overshadowed all of them, the two heroes of faith spoke with Jesus concerning His departure from Earth to heaven. The purpose of the transfiguration was to strengthen the firm resolve of Jesus as well as the hearts of His disciples. This incident also gave them a glimpse into their master's glory, for the hour of darkness was soon approaching. Peter utterly failed to grasp the significance of it all. He wanted to build three tabernacles and stay on the mountain. He simply had no understanding of the reason behind the event.

Coming down from the mountain, Jesus told Peter and the other two not to speak of what they had witnessed until after His death. I'm convinced He wanted them to see that when a marvelous spiritual experience takes place in our lives, it is important to understand that the experience is from the Lord and not always meant to be immediately shared. This tells us the Lord places great value on meekness and humility. He spoke through Isaiah these words,

> For this is what the high and lofty One says—he who lives forever, whose name is holy: "I live in a high and holy place, but also with the one who is contrite and lowly in spirit, to revive the spirit of the lowly and to revive the heart of the contrite."
>
> — Isaiah 57:15 (NIV)

And speaking of the humility of Jesus, Matthew 12:18–20 (NIV) says,

> Here is my servant whom I have chosen, the one I love, in whom I delight; I will put my Spirit on him, and he will proclaim justice to the nations. He will not quarrel or cry out; no one will hear his voice in the streets. A bruised reed he will not break, and a smoldering wick he will not snuff out, till he has brought justice through to victory.

Jesus' greatest illustration of humility occurred when, at the Last Supper, He removed His clothes, wrapped a towel around Himself, and then washed His disciples' feet. His graphic example again declared God's view of humility. Paul reiterated this viewpoint in Philippians 2:8 (NIV), "And being found in appearance as a man, he humbled himself by becoming obedient to death—even death on a cross!"

Author Rick Renner wrote this about the humility exhibited by Jesus,

> *The word* humbled *is the Greek word* tapeinao, *and it means* to be humble, to be lowly, *and* to be willing to stoop to any measure that is needed. *Think of the humility that would be required for God to shed His magnificent glory and lower Himself to become like a member of His own creation! Consider the greatness of God's love that drove Him to divest Himself of all His splendor and become like a man. This is precisely what occurred when Jesus left the majestic realms of Heaven. It is the true story of a King who traded His royal garments and took upon Himself the clothing of a servant. But the story doesn't stop there. Jesus loved us so much that He exchanged his royal garments for the clothing of a beggar!*[48]

What was the Father's response to the Son of God's humility and sacrifice? Paul said,

> *Therefore God exalted him to the highest place and gave him the name that is above every name, that at the name of Jesus every knee should bow, in heaven and on earth and under the earth, and every tongue*

acknowledge that Jesus Christ is Lord, to the glory of God the Father.

— Philippians 2:9–11 (NIV)

Hallelujah!

In the Old Testament, humility was seen as an essential characteristic of true piety. The man who is right with God is a humble man. His prophets were required to be humble. Why? Without humility, a prophet would accept the accolades for his prophecy for himself instead of giving the glory to God (see Balaam's example in Numbers 22). God humbles men to bring them to Himself, and it is when men humble themselves before Him then they are accepted (2 Chronicles 7:14). The Lord desires all men to "walk humbly with your God" (Micah 6:8, NIV).[49] Solomon spoke about humility in Proverbs 22:4 (NIV), "Humility is the fear of the LORD; its wages are riches and honor and life."

In the New Testament, humility is an essential part of our spiritual development. Christians are to clothe themselves with humility (1 Peter 5:5), do nothing out of selfish ambition or vain conceit, but in humility consider others first (Philippians 2:3), and show understanding and wisdom by living a good life filled with deeds done in humility (James 3:13).

In His teaching, Jesus preached that the exalted would be abased and the humble would be exalted (Luke 14:11), and anyone who humbled themselves as a little child, would be the greatest in the kingdom of heaven. In his last meeting with the Ephesian elders, Paul reminded them, "You know how I lived the whole time I was with you, from the first day I came into the province of Asia. *I served the Lord with great humility and with tears*" (Acts 20:18–19, NIV) (emphasis added by the author).

And the apostle included humility in his list of spiritual attributes to the Colossian church (Colossians 4:12).

Humility is at the root of all other graces and virtues. Self-exaltation spoils everything. Pride goes before destruction. There can be no real effective ministry without humility. Augustine said, "Humility is first, second and third in Christianity."[50] The first of the Beatitudes was to "the poor in spirit" (Matthew 5:3), and it was "the meek" who should "inherit the earth." Humility is the way to true greatness.[51]

Balanced with humility, Jesus, Moses, and Elijah are widely known for their great confidence. Consider the confidence it took for Jesus to lay down His life, for Moses to stand face to face with God, or for Elijah to confront the eight-hundred-fifty false prophets of Baal and Ashtoreth on Mount Carmel. The Bible teaches the value of confidence (Isaiah 30:15; Hebrews 10:35) in God (Psalm 65:5) and as revealed in Christ (Ephesians 3:12; 1 John 5:13–14).

The chief Hebrew word translated as "confidence" (*batach*) means, perhaps, radically, "to be open," showing that what originated the idea of "confidence;" reveals where there was nothing hidden, a person felt safe.[52] Jeremiah 17:7–8 (NIV) says,

> *But blessed is the one who trusts in the LORD, whose confidence is in him. They will be like a tree planted by the water that sends out its roots by the stream. It does not fear when heat comes; its leaves are always green. It has no worries in a year of drought and never fails to bear fruit.*

Joshua was told to have confidence (1 Joshua 1:8), and David exhibited his confidence when facing Goliath (1 Kings 17). Tremendous confidence in the Lord was exhibited through the stand the three Hebrews took when they refused to bow to Nebuchadnezzar's statue and were thrown into the fiery furnace (Daniel 3:15–18).

Christ's ministry illustrates His confidence through His prophetic ministry and office in the most extensive and exalted sense of the word. The first time we see His confidence occurred when Mary and Joseph found Him in the temple at the age of twelve. Upon finding Him in the temple, His parents, both worried and no doubt quite upset, questioned His actions. Luke writes,

After three days they found him in the temple courts, sitting among the teachers, listening to them and asking them questions. Everyone who heard him was amazed at his understanding and his answers. When his parents saw him, they were astonished. His mother said to him, "Son, why have you treated us like this? Your father and I have been anxiously searching for you." "Why were you searching for me?" he asked. "Didn't you know I had to be in my Father's house?"

— Luke 2:46–49 (NIV)

Jesus confidently spoke to John the Baptist about the need for Him to be baptized. Forty days later, He openly and confidently declared at the Synagogue in Capernaum,

"The Spirit of the Lord is on me, because he has anointed me to preach good news to the poor. He has

*sent me to proclaim freedom for the prisoners and
recovery of sight for the blind, to set the oppressed
free, to proclaim the year of the Lord's favor." Then he
rolled up the scroll, gave it back to the attendant and
sat down. The eyes of everyone in the synagogue were
fastened on him. He began by saying to them, "Today
this scripture is fulfilled in your hearing."*

— Luke 4:18–21 (NIV)

His intimate knowledge of God (John 16:15), the quality of His teaching (John 3), and the authority that He spoke with (John 1:9, 17–18) all rightly revealed His confidence in His calling and purpose. Jesus was unafraid to confront the religious Pharisees, especially when they were using their own traditions to denigrate others. Demons trembled at His confident words, and illness was no match for a confident word from His lips or the touch of His hand. By the acknowledgment of even those who have denied His divine nature and redemptive work, He continues to be recognized as never being willing to surrender to the circumstances, no matter how difficult. Whether multiplying loaves and fishes, walking on water, or standing before Pilate, Jesus stood confident in His source.

The confidence revealed in His teaching was remarkable! Whether a parable, proverb, absolute affirmation, suggestion, an allusion to simple objects, or when He made application to practical life—all of His teachings were powerful and yet easily understood. He challenged the status quo to the delight of the common people. He confounded the scribes and teachers of the law with His knowledge of the Scriptures. Even they had to admit He did not speak like one of them but as one who had authority! (Matthew 7:29).

In the book of Acts, the leaders of the Sanhedrin were amazed at the confidence of the Lord's two disciples, Peter and John. What was their opinion concerning their confidence? "These men had been with Jesus" (Acts 4:13, NIV).

Our lives should be full of His confidence. When we pray, we should do so with confidence. Hebrews 4:16 (NIV) says, "Let us then approach God's throne of grace with confidence, so that we may receive mercy and find grace to help us in our time of need." And concerning any spiritual attack, let us declare, "Though an host should encamp against me, my heart shall not fear: though war should rise against me, in this *will* I *be confident*" (Psalm 27:3, KJV) (emphasis added by the author). Having done all to stand, let us stand (Ephesians 6:11–14) and be "confident of this very thing, that he which hath begun a good work in you will perform it until the day of Jesus Christ" (Philippians 1:6, KJV).

When we pray, we should do so with confidence.

I love these words by John C. Maxwell in his book, *Leading in Tough Times*. He said, "In tough times the people we lead find out who we are, and we also find out what we're made of." As author Jack Kinder says,

> *You're not made in a crisis—you're revealed. When you squeeze an orange—you get orange juice. When you squeeze a lemon—you get lemon juice. When a human being gets squeezed—you get what is inside—positive or negative.*

The best way to approach tough times is to confidently see them as opportunities. Most people want their problems to be fixed without their having to face them, but that is usually not possible.

A balanced life of humility and confidence must be embraced. For us to "just make the decision" to do it is not enough. A balanced life of this kind must be rooted and grounded in love, built on having the mind of Christ, and established with a grateful attitude. Then, such humility and confidence can be revealed through the expectation that all the promises of God are *yes* and *amen*, in Christ Jesus!

CHAPTER THIRTEEN:

Honor and Submission

You are worthy, our Lord and God, to receive glory and honor and power, for you created all things, and by your will they were created and have their being.

— Revelation 4:11 (NIV)

Be devoted to one another in love. Honor one another above yourselves.

— Romans 12:10 (NIV)

Before we begin speaking directly about the manifestation and administration of the ministry of the Holy Spirit and the gift of prophecy, there are a couple of aspects concerning our preparation for the approaching prophetic outpouring that need to be addressed. If we are going to be effective and successful in the next outpouring of apostolic and prophetic ministry, we must add to our balance of humility and confidence the spiritual attributes of honor and submission.

To be frank, these are two concepts that are seldom addressed or even mentioned in the modern church age. They have been cast aside and replaced by the ideals of a "seeker-friendly" church.

To attract more people (which, by the way, isn't really working), the church has fallen for the world's values of selfishness (I want it my way) and self-interest (I want what is best for me). Such is revealed in the fact that Christians change churches as often as they change cell phones. The concept of the *golden rule* has faded out of the consciousness of this modern age. This is in stark contrast to the treasures that can be found in heaven and the life of Jesus. In His life on the earth, Jesus not only lived a balanced life of confidence and humility, as well as all the other attributes we have addressed, but He fully exhibited a life of honor and submission.

Webster's 1828 dictionary defines honor as,

> *To revere; to respect; to treat with deference and sub-mission, to reverence; to manifest the highest veneration for, in words and actions; to entertain the most exalted thoughts of; to worship; to adore. It also means any expression of respect or of high estimation by words or actions. Honor is true nobleness of mind; magnanimity; dignified respect for character, springing from probity, principle or moral rectitude; a distinguishing trait in the character of good men. Concerning one's view of God, it means reverence, adoration; or any act by which reverence and submission are expressed.[53]*

Jesus gave honor first and foremost to His Father (John 8:49). The word honor comes from the Greek word *timios*. It means to see a person as precious, esteemed, and especially dear. It is connected to the words *value* and *treasure*. The Scripture tells us to both honor and give honor to God (1 Timothy 1:17; Revelation

19:1). Giving God honor is more than the absence of our taking His Name in vain or offering Him praise with our words when our heart is far from Him (Isaiah 29:13). Honor is more than just the profession that one is a believer in Christ. Such describes only lip service.

Honor proceeds from a heart filled with God's love, a transformed mind, and found in those who have offered themselves to God with an attitude of thanksgiving, praise, and worship. The word honor represents more than mere outward religious activities or participation in a church service. Honor proceeds from our innermost being because of the value we see in the Lord and our relationship with Him. True honor does not prefer the devices and traditions of men but the giving of oneself totally and completely to God. It is best revealed through dedication and devotion, first and foremost, to the Lord.

Honor is best revealed through dedication and devotion.

The biblical idea behind giving honor to God, along with offering praise and worship to Him, comes from the Latin word *pretium*, which means "price" or "value" and should be defined as an ascription of value or worth. Thanksgiving, praise, and honor may be given to unworthy objects or with improper motives, but true honor can only be found in a sincere acknowledgment of a real conviction of worth. This includes the worth of that which has been received and when one acknowledges the worth of the Lord, to whom all glory and honor is due. In the book of Revelation, the adoration of God and the Lamb fills the highest heavens because God and the Lamb are "worthy" to be worshipped, honored, and praised.

A great example of biblical honor is found in the psalm written by Asaph at David's celebration of the ark of the covenant being brought into Jerusalem (1 Chronicles 16:7–30). And yet, David's honor of the Lord did not end at the celebration. David erected a tabernacle on Mount Zion where honor, thanksgiving, and worship flowed night and day for over forty years! Here is part of that wonderful hymn that was written to set the tone for what would become Earth's greatest and longest worship service.

> *For great is the LORD and most worthy of praise; he*
> *is to be feared above all gods. For all the gods of the*
> *nations are idols, but the LORD made the heavens.*
> *Splendor and majesty are before him; strength and joy*
> *in his dwelling place. Ascribe to the LORD, all you*
> *families of nations, ascribe to the LORD glory and*
> *strength. Ascribe to the LORD the glory due his name;*
> *bring an offering and come before him. Worship the*
> *LORD in the splendor of his holiness.*
>
> — 1 Chronicles 16:25–29 (NIV)

There is a restaurant in the Dallas-Fort Worth area that now requires honor to be a part of the dining experience they offer. The owner of the establishment recently told the news media that "this new idea" has put some off. To dine in his restaurant, a person must be willing to lock their phone in a case that will be placed in a secured box away from the dining area. Men must wear either a sport coat or suit jacket, and women must "dress with class." The restaurant also requests that one should expect the meal to take a couple of hours (no hurrying through dinner). When asked about these requirements and requests, the owner said he "wanted people to *honor* the time, enjoy the meal and each other's company."

On the other hand, most church services are now full of people *on their phones.* The things of God can be seen in many church services holding second place to sending or receiving texts. Many modern churches have now embraced the idea that people won't give up or even turn off their phones. No one thinks twice about someone being on their phone during praise or worship or even during the teaching segment of the service. While this may be attractive to the modern crowd, I wonder, does it give honor to God?

Giving honor to God must involve the element of time and attention, both of which should be focused on Him, His Word, and what He wants to do in and through us. When we are more focused on texting someone who is not in the church service, how can we effectively minister to those who are? As I have discussed concerning other attributes in this book, to institute honor into our lives, we must make room for it. Being consumed with this modern life (including our phones, the internet, and our work) is revealed by our focus on our wants, needs, and desires instead of focusing on the Lord and following Him.

The word honor (Hebrew *kabad*) means that another's life and words *carry weight* in ours. When giving honor, we are giving them a place in our life, showing that person with our words and actions that we value them, that they are important to us, and that we actually care about them. Paul restated this idea when he wrote about children showing honor to their parents in Ephesians 6:1–3. The apostle chose the Greek word *timao* when writing about honor. *Timao* means to show deference and reverence and to value another person by rank and state of the office that they hold.[54] In direct relation to this word is the reason why children should call their parents Father and Mother, or Mom and Dad, rather than by their given names. It is why if we show honor, we call our personal physician, *doctor*, or the president of the United States, *Mr. President*.

Giving honor to one's parents is the first commandment with promise. The commandment is part of the *ten commandments* (not suggestions) given from God through Moses to the nation of Israel in Exodus 20:12 (NIV), "Honor your father and your mother, so that you may live long in the land the LORD your God is giving you." Another commandment with promise is found in Proverbs 3:9–10 (NIV), "Honor the LORD with your wealth, with the firstfruits of all your crops; then your barns will be filled to overflowing, and your vats will brim over with new wine."

In John 5:22–23 (NIV), Jesus claimed the same right to be given the same honor and worship from men that His Father was to be given. Jesus said,

> *Moreover, the Father judges no one, but has entrusted all judgment to the Son, that all may honor the Son just as they honor the Father. Whoever does not honor the Son does not honor the Father, who sent him.*

In other words, showing dishonor to Jesus is to dishonor the Father who sent Him (also see John 8:49; 12:26; 15:23). There is a small comfort in these words for those who praise Jesus as a great teacher or prophet and yet deny His claims to be the Son of God or to be worshipped. The apostle John holds Jesus in high honor throughout his writings, but so do the other Gospels and the rest of the New Testament.[55]

We must not stop with our honor of God the Father and the Lord Jesus Christ. We are to honor the person of the Holy Spirit, His revelation, and gifts both revealed and administrated throughout our lives. Such is done by seeking to receive and understand that He has been sent to live within us and to administer the gifts of God. A great price was paid for our salvation, but the incident of our coming to Christ and being forgiven of both sin and sins was just the beginning. Paul exhorted the church in 1 Thessalonians 5:16–20 (NIV) to do more by…

> *Be joyful always; pray continually; give thanks in all circumstances, for this is God's will for you in Christ Jesus. Do not put out the Spirit's fire; do not treat prophecies with contempt.*

The concept of giving and showing honor must be extended to others. First to our parents, then to the elders that labor in the Word and doctrine (1 Timothy 5:17), as well as other followers of Christ (Romans 12:10). Each of us should show honor and respect to others, as unto the Lord. Giving honor to whom honor is due means that we first give others the lead and both recognize and honor God's gifts in them. It means to prefer and respect others in all the various relationships we have in life. Paul's writings are full of exhortations that children should show proper respect to their parents, parents to children, servants to their masters, etc., and for all to strive by mutual kindness to promote the happiness of the Christian community.[56]

How opposite this is from the spirit of the world; the spirit which seeks, not to confer honor, but to only obtain it; which aims, not to diffuse respect, but to attract all others to give honor to us. As self-importance consumes our society, it is quickly bringing an end to honor and causing an explosion of envy, self-ambition, and dissatisfaction. Honor produces contentment, harmony, love, and order in the community, while selfishness creates more crime, strife, discord, and malice. We must pray for and work to establish honor again in the church. It would humble the ambition of those who love to have pre-eminence and make every man willing to occupy the place for which God has designed him.[57]

Honor produces contentment, harmony, love, and order.

Along with the giving and showing of honor, it is necessary to develop an attitude of submission to God and to those who have been put in our lives to oversee and mentor us. Submission is the brother of humility. James said, "'God opposes the proud but shows favor to the humble.' Submit yourselves, then, to God. Resist the devil, and he will flee from you. Come near to God and he will come near to you" (James 4:6–8, NIV).

In Luke 7:6–9 (NIV), a Roman centurion who had come to Jesus to request the healing of his servant said,

> *"Lord, don't trouble yourself, for I do not deserve to have you come under my roof. That is why I did not even consider myself worthy to come to you. But say the word, and my servant will be healed. For I myself am a man under authority [in submission], with soldiers under me. I tell this one, 'Go,' and he goes; and that one, 'Come,' and he comes. I say to my servant, 'Do*

this,' and he does it." When Jesus heard this, he was amazed at him, and turning to the crowd following him, he said, "I tell you, I have not found such great faith even in Israel."

The Lord reiterated this understanding when He answered the Pharisees in John 7:16 (NIV), "My teaching is not my own. It comes from the one who sent me."

The apostle Peter, in his letter to the churches of Asia Minor, said,

In the same way, you who are younger, submit yourselves to your elders. All of you, clothe yourselves with humility toward one another, because, "God opposes the proud but shows favor to the humble." Humble yourselves, therefore, under God's mighty hand, that he may lift you up in due time.

— 1 Peter 5:5–6 (NIV)

And Paul wrote, "Submit to one another out of reverence for Christ" (Ephesians 5:21, NIV).

In all these scriptural examples, the word *submission* comes from the Greek word *hupotaso*. *Hupotaso* is an old military term meaning to "line up under" (Colossians 3:18).[58] The primary point of each of these examples is to show that when it comes to embracing and living the spiritual values of the kingdom of God, the self must be dethroned. God must be exalted, and consequently, honor and submission must be offered toward other fellow Christians. This view is in harmony with the humble spirit of the gospel. Pride leads us to demand rigorously from others what we fancy or what we consider they owe us; humility is to give to others what Christ teaches that we owe to them.[59]

SECTION THREE:

Embracing and Enjoying the Process

I t is now time to turn our focus on what I believe to be the elements of the impending wave of the Spirit. So far, we have learned that, to be able to fully embrace this next move of God, we must grow and change.

The development of new attitudes and habits will require alert monitoring to ensure their continuity. Old beliefs, attitudes, and habits will try to reassert themselves if we are not vigilant. We must choose to develop a plan before the old way of thinking arises for dealing with it, should such occur.

I want to share this quote from Paul J. Meier again. He said,

> *Many people live their lives in the shadow of public opinion, drifting with the tide of criticism, and wind-up wallowing in the backwash of mediocrity. Remember, no one can determine your desires, needs, or wants because no one else knows your priority of values or understands your potential. Be determined to have firm resolve, quiet confidence, and unshakable*

persistence. You will never go any higher than you are right now unless you dare to be numbered among the few who march to the beat of different drums—the drums that beat within you!

Those whose lives you touch in the future will learn that spiritual knowledge, understanding, and wisdom flow from the heart of God into us and from us into others. The only meaningful motivation for this must be godly motivation based on the attitude and positive expectancy that flows out of the conviction that God has given us a hope and a future (Jeremiah 29:11).

CHAPTER FOURTEEN:

Revelational Knowledge and Prophetic Insight

But Moses replied, "Are you jealous for my sake? I wish that all the LORD's people were prophets and that the LORD would put his Spirit on them!"

— Numbers 11:29 (NIV)

However, as it is written: "What no eye has seen, what no ear has heard, and what no human mind has conceived"—the things God has prepared for those who love him— these are the things God has revealed to us by his Spirit. The Spirit searches all things, even the deep things of God.

— 1 Corinthians 2:9–10 (NIV)

Paul's foundation for his view of revelational knowledge and prophetic insight is found in these two scriptures. Like Moses, the apostle Paul wanted all of God's people to be illuminated to the value, both individually and collectively, of revelational knowledge and prophetic ministry. I believe that if we do not come to understand Paul's teaching about this, we will be relegated to an undervalued and underperforming life and ministry.

From the revelation given to him by the Holy Spirit, Paul spoke in 1 Corinthians 2 from the prophet Isaiah's prophecy, chapter sixty-four and verse six. He reiterated to the believers at Corinth that none of the rulers of this age could or would ever be able to understand the things of God. For if they had, they would not have crucified the Lord of glory. And, along with rulers of this age, no mortal man or woman in themselves has ever seen or their mind conceived, neither has it entered their heart, the things God has prepared for those who love Him. But God. *But God has revealed it by His Spirit. Revealed what? Revealed what no eye can see, no ear can hear, and no human mind can conceive. What are these things? The deep things of God.*

I have heard many people and preachers in my lifetime quote Isaiah 64:6. Most have used it to say that no one (even believers) can really know about the things God has prepared for the people of God. They apparently never read the verses written by Paul to the Corinthians. I can promise you those who spoke such things had little spiritual insight and, for the most part, ignored the part where Paul said, "These things had been revealed to us [Paul and the others in his company]."

God prepared very special things for every person, for every church, and for every ministry.

Before the beginning of time, God preplanned and prepared the future. And, as I have mentioned before, I was there. You were there. We all were there, in Him. In that same moment, God prepared very special things for every person, for every church, and for every ministry. But the only access to those things is the revelational knowledge and prophetic insight given by the Holy Spirit. Such is like having a wonderful patron who has gone before you to set a table and prepare a meal. Because you were not involved in the planning, you could not know what the table would look like or what was going to be prepared. But then, prior to your arrival, your guest chooses to send you a picture to show you the gorgeous table and the luscious food that had been prepared and is awaiting your arrival.

Like that patron, God has something very special prepared for your future. It's important today that you get a revelation of what it is. In that same passage, Paul went on to say that anyone without the Spirit does not accept the things that come from the Spirit of God, for they are foolishness to him. Such things cannot be understood because they are spiritually discerned. To understand such things, we must have the mind of Christ. What was in God's mind in the beginning? The future. What did He speak? History in reverse. He knew the beginning from the end.

> *He has made everything beautiful in its time. He has also set eternity in the human heart; yet no one can fathom what God has done from beginning to end. …Whatever is has already been, and what will be has been before; and God will call the past to account.*
>
> — Ecclesiastes 3:11, 15 (NIV)

I want you to read the next few paragraphs very slowly as I do my best to explain the revelational knowledge God gave me concerning Solomon's insight.

Solomon's knowledge and insights are called prophetic revelation or revelational knowledge. *It is to speak the things of the future things in their present tense.* Or to speak the things one does not know through the illumination and revelation of God. Solomon said, "Whatever is has already been, and what will be has been before." When God said, "Let there be light." Most people think that the text is speaking of our sun being created and that its light began shining from the beginning of time (think Genesis) and is continuing to shine down through time to the end (think Revelation). But the word *light* comes from a Hebrew root meaning *to illumine. The light spoken of was created before the sun, and our solar system was created.* Solomon was given spiritual knowledge as to the direction that God's light shines. (His revelational knowledge and prophetic revelation.)

When God spoke light into existence, He began where He always does, at the end. *He knows the beginning from the end, plans the beginning from the* end, *and prepares the beginning from the end.*

Therefore, the light God created on that first day shines from the end (think the book of Revelation) backward through time all the way to the beginning (think Genesis). This would mean the closer mankind comes to the end of time, the greater and brighter the illumination or light. The closer we come to the end of chronological time, the brighter the light or prophetic illumination and revelational knowledge. I also now understand that the light spoken into existence by God and recorded in Genesis is not limited to spiritual understanding. Over the last two hundred years and fifty years (since the major prophetic shift that happened during the great awakening), we have seen tremendous advancements in medicine, technology, communications, science, and a multiplicity of things too numerous to mention. These were enhanced around the time of the start of the Pentecostal Movement in 1901 and have been exploding since the beginning of the healing and Latter Rain movement in the 1940s and 1950s.

Since then, humanity has experienced a new level of knowledge and understanding. There are inventions, like the silicone computer chip, happening almost every day. Therefore, we in the church should expect the same. Instead, most of the church continues to be mired in the revelational knowledge of the past. Yes, the Great Reformation moved the church from Catholicism to the understanding that we are saved by faith in the Lord Jesus Christ, not works. And what followed was that understanding of every type exploded between the First and Second Great Awakenings (1720s–1840s).

Advancements in evangelism multiplied exponentially during the same times of the Holiness, Pentecostal, and Charismatic movements. In each spiritual reformation, the church came to know, understand, and experience God in wonderfully fresh and exciting ways. But should we be content with where we now find ourselves? *No!* And again, I say, *No!*

The church must again become open to having our lives overwhelmed by Him.

The church must again become open to having our lives overwhelmed by Him who seeks to fully reveal Himself and to pour everything He has prepared for us into our lives. Through the Spirit's revelational knowledge and prophetic illumination, we can and should encounter Him beyond our current understanding of the mysteries in Christ. What we now believe was indescribable and incomprehensible to those in the past. Why?

Because the light was not as bright as it is now. Therefore, what *has been has become familiar to us.*

It is the example of the cell phone. Those who lived before the time the telephone was created (around 1880) could not have begun to comprehend a device that has the abilities our cell phones have. God's light and voice will disclose (to those who will receive it) what He has prepared (in the future) for those that love Him. God is not just some idea. He is not an enigma. He is the one and only God. He is wonderful and marvelous! His ways are above our ways, and His thoughts are above our thoughts (Isaiah 55:9). He desires to reveal to us His ways and thoughts.

He is to whom we are accountable, but also the pattern for our lives. He seeks to be known, yes fully known by those who love Him and are willing to have their understanding opened (Luke 24:45). A servant does not know his master's business, but a son receives full information (Galatians 4:1–7). He is our heavenly Father, the God of Abraham. He is the Son of God, the Lord Jesus Christ, who is the first and last, the beginning and the end! He desires to illumine and reveal to us new dimensions of Himself and His glory!

As His light has shined backward through chronological time, the cross stands as the crisis point of human history. And, where it stands, makes the light (shining backward through time) cast a shadow of the cross into the Old Testament. While many are teaching today that the Old Testament is irrelevant to the modern church, one of the ways the Holy Spirit desires to reveal the very best of Christ's kingdom is through the types and shadows found there. The description of such was used by Paul in Colossians 2:17 to denote the typical relation of the Jewish to the Christian dispensation.

An example is the pattern of the tabernacle given to Moses (Hebrews 8:5). Each part of the tabernacle is a shadow or type representing a real part of the kingdom of God. Like an onion, what we see on the surface (the first meaning—which was given at that time) is understated. God chooses to use both descriptive and indicative words in the types and shadows of the Old Testament. While His language may seem mysterious at times, His revelation to us concerning the types and shadows of the Old Testament is distinctive.

The desire for revelational knowledge and prophetic understanding should cause us to seek His face and turn from our own thinking, so we can hear from heaven (1 Chronicles 7:14). We must pray for Him to bring illumination and revelation to the body of Christ. For without it, most churches will continue to have structure and organization, but the life once enjoyed will begin to be swallowed up (if it hasn't already) by the traditions of men.

The Hebrew word translated as "prophet" (beginning with Samuel) was *ro'eh*. It means to have *spiritual and prophetic insight*. Samuel, Elisha, and Isaiah were all called *ro'eh* in the Old Testament because they were *seers*. They had the ability to see into the realm of the Spirit (and the future) and see what other people could not see. In 2 Kings chapter six, we find this example,

> *When the servant of the man of God got up and went out early the next morning, an army with horses and chariots had surrounded the city. "Oh no, my lord! What shall we do?" the servant asked. "Don't be afraid," the prophet answered. "Those who are with us are more than those who are with them." And Elisha*

prayed, "Open his eyes, LORD, so that he may see." *Then the LORD opened the servant's eyes, and he looked and saw the hills full of horses and chariots of fire all around Elisha.*

— 2 Kings 6:15–17 (NIV)
(emphasis added by the author)

When the Lord opened the servant's eyes that day, Elisha's servant was able to see what Elisha saw and look beyond the natural army and see God's army! Yes, the enemy had surrounded the city. But when his eyes were opened, the servant saw the army of heaven surrounding the enemy, and that victory was sure! Hallelujah! Elisha knew what the apostle John knew before John said it; *that greater is He that is within us than he that is the world.* He also came to know what Isaiah would come to know, *that no weapon formed against us will prosper.* He then knew the revelational knowledge that was given to Paul some 800 years later, "If God is for us, who can be against us?" (1 John 4:4; Isaiah 54:17; Romans 8:31, NIV).

Paul told the Corinthian Christians that God's revelational knowledge and insight produce not only the ability to see but to hear. Again, going back to the prophet Samuel. In 1 Samuel 3:4–7, we find the call of Samuel to the ministry. One night as Samuel was lying on his bed, he heard a voice. Thinking it was his mentor, Eli, Samuel went running to Eli's bedroom. Samuel asked to know what Eli wanted of him in the middle of the night; Eli's response was that he had not called Samuel's name and that the young lad should go back and lay on his bed. He also instructed Samuel that if he heard the voice again to ask the voice, who are you?

Eli had correctly discerned the situation. God was speaking to Samuel for the first time. Samuel (the seer) was hearing God's voice for the first time. That night Samuel heard a voice that only Samuel could hear. Both spiritual illumination and revelational knowledge can and will bring us a similar experience. (Remember what I mentioned earlier concerning *spiritual déjà vu*.) It is like watching a replay of a sporting event that has already been completed and that you have watched before. It is like knowing the future before it exists in chronological time. And each time you watch a replay of that sporting event, you know even more about what's going to take place—before it happens. Why? Because you've seen it before.

Prophetic people have open eyes and open ears. In the book of Revelation, Jesus said to John, "Whoever has ears, let them hear what the Spirit says to the churches" (Revelation 2:7, 17, NIV). God is still speaking! We must become open to His voice! We must become open to seeing as He sees!

Another Old Testament word that is translated, prophet, is the Hebrew word *nabiy'*. *Nabiy'* is from the root *naaba'*, which means "to bubble forth as a fountain." (See Psalm 45:1 (KJV), "My heart is inditing up a good matter," namely, inspired by the Holy Spirit.)[60]

In other words, as likened to an artesian well, when revelational knowledge and spiritual illumination are given to us, we cannot stop it from bubbling up within us. And when He speaks to us, He usually is doing so because He desires to speak through us. He wants us to see, hear and speak to those whom God has connected us with because His understanding is not just for us but for those He has put within our lives. He does this so that we will be blessed and be the avenue of His blessing to others! (See Genesis 12:2.)

Jeremiah spoke of his receiving the illuminating light of God into his heart and his soul. He said it was like *fire burning in his bones*. Such is like one putting their thumb over the end of a water hose that has been turned on. You can hold back the water pressure for a while, but sooner or later, the water is going to come out! John the Baptist described himself as a *voice crying in the wilderness*. When He saw Jesus coming to be baptized, he had heard and knew the moment he saw Jesus that Jesus was the one the Spirit had already spoken to him about. John called Him "the Lamb of God, who takes away the sin of the world" (John 1:29, NIV). How did he know this? Like Jeremiah, he saw what he could not see, heard what he could not hear, and said what no one else was able to say.

Each of these examples describes a supernatural experience. It cannot be explained. It can only be experienced. Even in my sad attempt to explain it, I cannot really describe or clarify it to you because such spiritual revelation and illumination must be experienced. Such is outside of the natural realm of our existence. It is a heavenly treasure put into an earthen vessel. Paul said, "But we have this treasure in jars of clay to show that this all-surpassing power is from God and not from us" (2 Corinthians 4:7, NIV).

The prophet Isaiah described his first prophetic experience in Isaiah chapter six, which says,

> In the year that King Uzziah died, I saw the Lord,
> high and exalted, seated on a throne; and the train of
> his robe filled the temple. Above him were seraphim,
> each with six wings: With two wings they covered their

faces, with two they covered their feet, and with two they were flying. And they were calling to one another: "Holy, holy, holy is the LORD Almighty; the whole earth is full of his glory." At the sound of their voices the doorposts and thresholds shook and the temple was filled with smoke. "Woe to me!" I cried. "I am ruined! For I am a man of unclean lips, and I live among a people of unclean lips, and my eyes have seen the King, the LORD Almighty."

— Isaiah 6:1–5 (NIV)

The year King Uzziah died, Isaiah's prophetic revelation and ministry began. Why? I believe it was in that year the good king whom Isaiah had grown to know and love was being moved off the scene. No doubt, it was a time of frustration and questioning for the young prophet. Uzziah had been a good king and had reigned for fifty-two years, which was longer than Isaiah had been alive. His name, Uzziah, means "My strength is Jehovah." And it was in that year of great turmoil that the king died. It was also the year Isaiah had his heavenly vision. *He saw 'Adonay, the wonderful, awesome, and glorious Lord.* 'Adonay is a Hebrew Name for God and was only spoken in place of the name *Yahweh* when the Name was to be greatly celebrated and given great reverence.

Isaiah saw 'Adonay high and lifted up. His train literally filled the heavenly palace. Isaiah saw a wonderous and holy place full of glory. The vision gave Isaiah insight into the celestial home of the Lord God Jehovah, filled with all His splendor, glory, and power. Andrew Maclaren put it this way,

When the earthly king was laid in the grave; the prophet saw that the true King of Israel was neither the dead Uzziah nor the young Jotham, but the Lord of hosts. *And, seeing that, fears and forebodings and anxieties and the sense of loss, all vanished; and new strength came to Isaiah. He went into the temple laden with anxious thoughts; he came out of it with a springy step and a lightened heart.*[61]

Isaiah also saw angelic beings called *seraphim*. He heard them declaring to each other, "Holy, holy, holy is the LORD Almighty; the whole earth is full of his glory" (Isaiah 6:3, NIV). Next, Isaiah saw himself, first in comparison to the Lord of glory and then to the people that were in his life. He was illuminated to his sin and the sin of his people. And finally, Isaiah saw the heavenly altar with coals of holy fire upon it. He saw one of the seraphim taking one of the coals off the altar and touching his lips. He then heard from heaven, "See, this has touched your lips; your guilt is taken away and your sin atoned for" (Isaiah 6:7, NIV). With his sin purged and sin taken away, Isaiah declared that he was ready and willing to be sent (as a word from the Lord) to those people that were in his life and nation (think sentence, paragraph, and chapter of life). That experience led to a highly regarded and recognized prophetic ministry, which brought about a new and dynamic shift in the ministry then and has continued down through the ages.

My own first experience happened many years ago. At the end of an evening church service, I went with my dad to pray at the front of the church. As I was praying, I saw people in a rainforest. In the rainforest, I saw a clearing. I saw four gas lamps on four poles and a group of about one hundred people. Then, I saw a young adult man preaching and then several people responding by coming forward to give their hearts to God. They did not speak English, and I did not understand the language that they were speaking.

My heart broke for those people. For several years after that initial experience, the Holy Spirit brought that picture before me. I sought the Lord again and again for those people. I prayed to have the opportunity to minister to them. I could not forget what I saw or heard, and I couldn't forget them. Many years passed, and in 1985, I led a team to construct a church in Honduras. The attending missionary asked if I would be willing to go out with him to preach near the Guatemalan border. We drove for several hours, and when we arrived, we were in a rainforest. At first, I didn't pay any attention to it. I was busy talking to the missionary. Suddenly, we were in a clearing. And I still didn't pay any attention. People began to gather. Our crusade service began, and as planned, I stepped forward to preach. As I was preaching, the missionary began interpreting. The crowd continued to grow. More and more people came.

And, when I came to the end of the message, the Holy Spirit stepped right in. He reopened my spiritual eyes. I felt led to walk to the edge of the rainforest, and as I turned around, there were four poles with four lamps. I saw several people coming forward. They were the people I had seen years before. It was the people from the vision. That night I truly understood how valuable all people are to God. I understood that the Holy Spirit will show us the future in the present.

Why? God the Father has given His only begotten Son for the salvation of the whole world. The Holy Spirit was promised and sent into the hearts of those who have accepted the revelation of Jesus Christ. Many years before this example happened in real time, the Holy Spirit revealed to me what He wanted to do and did do in the lives of those people. God had illuminated my heart and given me revelational knowledge. He gave me the burden to intercede for those people for years and ordered my steps to that certain place at the perfect time, to those particular people, with a specific message. This happened because of *their value to Him!* Each of those Honduran men and women were very poor and uneducated. They were seen as having nothing and being of little value—as far as the world was concerned. But to God, they were His valuables. He wanted them to fill them with heaven's valuable treasure and become His vault filled with His glory! Hallelujah!

This kind of treasure cannot be explained, only experienced. More glorious than precious stones are the blessings of our Lord! More precious than gold and silver is the deposit of His eternal treasure in our earthen vessel. He continues to reveal and fill us with the treasures of heaven. We must give glory to His Name. He is worthy of all praise, glory, and worship. I encourage you to now seek His face. Ask Him for what purpose did He take hold of you. Ask Him for revelational knowledge and spiritual illumination so that you, too, may be introduced to the deep things of God. Start today!

CHAPTER FIFTEEN:

Spiritual Understanding

For this cause we also, since the day we heard it, do not cease to pray for you, and to desire that ye might be filled with the knowledge of his will in all wisdom and spiritual understanding.

— Colossians 1:9 (KJV)

One of the major roles of both Old and New Testament prophets was to have spiritual understanding. Paul's prayer and desire for the Colossians were no doubt based on his concern for the growing Gnosticism the Colossians were facing. According to the Gnostics, God is thought of as an ultimate, nameless, unknowable being.[62] Therefore, there is no place in Gnosticism either for the creation of the universe by a real God or for the incarnation and work of Christ.[63] This is in direct contrast to the spiritual understanding given to the apostle Paul (Ephesians 1:17–19) and these words from the apostle John's letter to the churches of Asia Minor.

We know also that the Son of God has come and has given us understanding [diannoian], so that we may know [hina ginoskomen] *him who is true. And we are in him who is true by being in his Son Jesus Christ. He is the true God and eternal life.*

— 1 John 5:20 (NIV)

Spiritual understanding is real, living, and will always be revelatory to the moment and progressive toward the future (see 2 Peter 1:12). The more we come to understand Christ Jesus, the more we grow to be like Him and the closer we become to Him.

The more we come to understand Christ Jesus, the more we grow to be like Him. Our spiritual lives are destined for endless pilgrimage, not a comfortable destination. It is as though our salvation brought us to a gigantic spiritual land, and we are called to be pressing deeper and deeper into the wonders of His grace. Many are only willing to only go "so far." But in this book, I am encouraging you to seek to learn and always be learning more and more of Him.

Since the Reformation, all the Protestant denominations have been built on the foundation of the revelational knowledge and spiritual understanding that was revealed to a certain person or group of people at a certain time. These revelations gave generations of people *spiritual light*. That light was given for the sake of them being enabled by the Holy Spirit to have a better understanding of Christ Jesus. The problem most of these Protestant denominations now have is they continue to stay stuck in the revelational knowledge given in the past. They are so connected to one particular person (example: Luther) or generation (example: Pentecostal) or method (example: Methodist) that they are unwilling to proceed into the knowledge given to subsequent generations. One such example has been the lack of understanding concerning the prophetic ministry of women, as mentioned in 2 Kings 22:14–15 (NIV) and Romans 16:7 (NIV).

> *Hilkiah the priest, Ahikam, Akbor, Shaphan and Asaiah went to speak to the prophet Huldah, who was the wife of Shallum son of Tikvah, the son of Harhas, keeper of the wardrobe. She lived in Jerusalem, in the New Quarter. She said to them, "This is what the LORD, the God of Israel, says."*

And,

> *Greet Andronicus and Junia [meaning "youthful" and, with little doubt, a woman's name], my fellow Jews who have been in prison with me. They are outstanding among the apostles [marked or stamped as a coin and counted among the apostles in the general sense true of Barnabas, James, the brother of Christ, Silas, and others], and they were in Christ before I was.*

Unwilling to accept new understanding, many women have been regulated to following the cultural example set in the book of 1 Corinthians, which was Paul's social solution for the Corinthian women who were speaking out loud to one another during the teaching of the Word of God. Paul told them they were to be silent (see 1 Corinthians 14:34). A lack of spiritual understanding has kept many Christian women, for the most part, silent in church. But thankfully, many women like Kathryn Kuhlman, Dr. Clarice Fluitt, and Beth Moore have taken note of these verses, embraced the call of God, and even embraced the life and understanding found in another of Paul's letters. To the Galatians, he wrote, "There is neither Jew nor Gentile, neither slave nor free, nor is there male and female, for you are all one in Christ Jesus" (Galatians 3:28, NIV).

It has taken hundreds of years for the organized church to recognize that God raised up women like Huldah and Junias to be full of spiritual wisdom and understanding. Several other women in the Bible are also mentioned as being prophetic, including eighty-four-year-old Anna, who worshipped day and night in the Jerusalem temple, fasting and praying. Eight days after Jesus' birth, Jesus was presented in the temple. Anna came to Mary and Joseph, giving thanks to God and speaking to them with her spiritual wisdom and understanding about the child as well as to all who were looking forward to redemption (Luke 2:36–38).

In Christ, there is neither male nor female, Jew nor Greek, black nor white, red nor yellow. God has chosen to…

> *Speak a message of wisdom among the mature, but not*
> *the wisdom of this age or of the rulers of this age, who*
> *are coming to nothing. No, we declare God's wisdom,*
> *a mystery that has been hidden and that God destined*
> *for our glory before time began.*
>
> — 1 Corinthians 2:6–7 (NIV)

E. Earle Ellis, a former research professor of Theology Emeritus and scholar in residence at Southwestern Baptist Theological Seminary, wrote several books about the workings and administration of spiritual understanding in the early church. In his book, *Prophecy and Hermeneutic in Early Christianity*, Ellis used an unusual word to describe those who have been blessed with spiritual wisdom and understanding (prophecy). He uses the word *pneumatic*. According to Ellis, *pneumatics* were early Christians who were characterized by spiritual gifts of inspired speech, divine discernment, and spiritual understanding. Many of which were coworkers of Paul and were engaged in preaching and teaching. He notes that the *pneumatics* were involved in the formulation of Christian theology (New Testament), and their insight into the Old Testament included their exposition and application of Old Testament Scripture. Dr. Ellis suggests some new directions for understanding history and the understanding of spiritual things, especially as it relates to prophecy and prophetic gifts.

How important is spiritual understanding? First Corinthians 12:1 speaks to the need for believers not to be ignorant of spiritual things. In the New Testament, ignorance is described in the Greek word *agnoia*, meaning "to have an absence of knowledge" (Acts 3:17; 17:30; Ephesians 4:18; 1 Peter 1:14). The Lord does not want us to be ignorant and think like the unsaved or even spiritual children (carnal believers). We have an anointing within us, and that anointing will teach us all things if we allow Him to. First John 2:20 (NIV) says, "But you have an anointing from the Holy One, and all of you know the truth." And 1 John 2:27 (NIV) states,

> As for you, the anointing you received from him
> remains in you, and you do not need anyone to teach
> you. But as his anointing teaches you about all things
> and as that anointing is real, not counterfeit—just as it
> has taught you, remain in him.

Paul taught the Corinthians (see chapters 12–14 of his first epistle to them) that when believers gather for corporate worship, each person should come expecting the prophetic ministry of the Holy Spirit to take place. Such should happen through those whom He has chosen, gifted, and is enabling. Paul instructed them to be prepared to either have a hymn, a word of instruction, a revelation, a tongue, or an interpretation. Why? Because the glorious treasure within us is to be shared with others. Like one of the eight parts of speech, some of us are called to be, act, modify, or interject. We are called to be people of value and add value to others as the Lord continues to illuminate and illustrate His treasures to us.

Every time we come to the house (think people, not building) of God, what is each of us supposed to do? We're supposed to come prepared to minister and to make room for His ministry to us, in us, and through us. Sadly, there are now few places where this kind of worship occurs. What has happened to it? Our understanding has faded away.

We have become time-bound, worldly-educated, entertainment-based, and consumed with the natural organization of things instead of following the order of God. Like the experience of Mary and Joseph, there is no room in the inn. No room for spiritual fathers to impart their knowledge to younger believers. No room for spiritual adolescents to learn so they can grow up. No, instead, many who speak from today's pulpits continue to rehash the elementary truths of God listed in Hebrews 6:1–2.

In most churches, there is no room for believers to learn how to see, hear, and speak the things of God. No, instead, many followers of Christ have now resorted to searching the internet for their spiritual instruction, taking the words of someone they have no real knowledge of or relationship with, and taking what they read on the internet as total truth. Many are taking the theological opinions of strangers or those who have great online reviews instead of participating in a prophetic community of people whose heart is set fully on the things of God.

I can see a shift coming. In the past, many in the church have become *stuck*, but I see that we should expect fresh bread from heaven, fresh understanding, and dynamic apostolic and prophetic ministries to be raised up. As one of my friends recently put it, what is coming will not take God's people to the next level but to a new dimension. I believe that! You should "enlarge the place of your tent, stretch your tent curtains wide, do not hold back; lengthen your cords, strengthen your stakes" (Isaiah 54:2, NIV). Furthermore, let us follow Paul's exhortation to the Galatians, "Since we live by the Spirit, let us keep in step with the Spirit" (Galatians 5:25, NIV).

Let us devote ourselves to possessing an insatiable hunger for the things of God.

Let us pray to become mediators and instructors of spiritual knowledge, inspired understanding, and wisdom of the Scriptures. Let us devote ourselves to possessing an insatiable hunger for the things of God. We have not received the spirit of the world but the Spirit who is from God, that we may understand what God has freely given us. We should speak not in words taught us by human wisdom but in words taught by the Spirit, expressing spiritual truths in spiritual words (see 1 Corinthians 2:12–13). How can we receive such wisdom and understanding? As I shared earlier about opening our hearts and minds, we must open ourselves up to the pouring forth of His glory.

Several years ago, I was led by the Holy Spirit to enter a time of extended fasting and praying. During that time, I was again reading the works of E. Earle Ellis. This time I was reading his book *Prophecy and Hermeneutic in Early Christianity*. Professor Ellis' exposition of the letters of Paul really inspired me to seek for a greater dimension of spiritual understanding. Over the next several weeks and months, I spent much time in prayer and fasting, just as Jesus directed His disciples in Matthew 17:21 (KJV), "Howbeit this kind goeth not out but by prayer and fasting." I experienced a very special season in the Lord. Several days into that special season, the Holy Spirit led me to study Paul's letter to the Colossians. As I began studying the second chapter, I felt encouraged to pray for what Paul said was "the full riches of complete understanding, in order that they may know the mystery of God, namely, Christ, in whom are hidden all the treasures of wisdom and knowledge" (Colossians 2:2–3, NIV).

I also prayed to be given insight concerning what A. W. Robertson said about these verses. Robertson said, "Paul desires the full use of the intellect in grasping the great mystery of Christ and it calls for the full and balanced exercise of all one's mental powers."[64] He went on to say that "Christ is 'the mystery of God,' but no longer hidden, but manifested [1 Corinthians 2:7] and *meant for us to know Christ to the fullness* [Greek: *pleroma*] of our capacity."[65]

The word fullness (*pleroma*) comes from the Greek word *pleroo*, which means to make full, to fill up, i.e., to fill to the full. The word was first used by the Greeks to describe a ship that had a full complement of men and supplies. Fullness enabled them to reach the port to which they were sailing. In other words, I was given the understanding that God desires that all of us be completely open before Him so that our spiritual understanding is filled and we are able to reach our destiny. He desires for us to abound in spiritual understanding. We are to be furnished and supplied liberally to the point of having spiritual understanding that is continually being completed in Him. Then we will be constantly being filled to the brim and running over.

A few days later, I was directed again by the Holy Spirit. I felt I was made to know that I was to fly from where my wife and I were ministering in New Mexico to Wichita, Kansas, so that I could pray for my dad's sister, who was dying of cancer. I was sitting on the plane praying about the situation when *I saw her in the hospital.* I do not know if I saw an actual vision or saw her in my spirit. But I saw (by the Spirit) my aunt and the family gathered around her. I noticed that there were two family members not there and wondered if what I saw was real. I felt that way because the two family members, whom I did not see, were the very ones who should have been at the hospital all the time.

When my cousin picked up my dad (who flew in from Idaho) and me, we drove straight from the airport to the hospital. He encouraged us with the news that several people were gathering at the church she attended for the purpose of praying for God to heal her. As he spoke, the Presence of God filled the automobile. I sensed something very special was happening. When we entered her hospital room an hour later, I knew that I had been there before (as I mentioned earlier). And, as I tried to explain earlier in this book, I felt a kind *of spiritual déjà vu.* Two of the family members, just as I had seen, were not there when we arrived. But there was me, my dad, my cousin, and another cousin gathered around my aunt, who was lying in bed, wearing the very pajamas I had "seen" on the plane.

I told my aunt I was there to pray and that the Lord had spoken to me on the plane. The moment I laid my hands on her, the glory of God filled the room. It was truly amazing. For almost an hour, waves of His Presence washed over us. We experienced heaven on Earth. The worship and tears flowed. The glory of God became stronger and stronger. Our voices became louder and louder, but no one came from the nurse's station to quiet us. No nurse or doctor even checked on us for more than an hour. At her church, a few miles away, something special was also happening. We learned later that the Holy Spirit was moving in a dynamic way among the people who had gathered to pray.

At the end of that hour, I felt directed to tell her to get up out of bed, and I helped her up (like the man at the Gate Beautiful in Acts 3). My aunt stood, and immediately, strength flowed into her body. Though usually a very quiet woman, she began praising, shouting, and even dancing. The doctors later confirmed that the cancer was completely gone; she was healed and made whole without their help! Glory to God! My aunt went on to live many, many more years. The spiritual understanding given to me had produced faith for God's healing power to manifest in my aunt's life that night. My aunt, myself, and all of us in the room were never the same. Hallelujah!

As all of us begin to experience the revealed mysteries of the approaching shift in the Spirit, it is imperative that we recognize we have been chosen and summoned, invited, appointed, adopted, and endowed by God to be His sons and daughters. It is also important that we understand "that we have come to the kingdom for such a time as this" (see Esther 4:14).

I have no doubt that the anointings of King David will give you even more spiritual understanding about these things. In

David's life, there were three anointings that took place. Each time David was anointed, he moved to a higher dimension of spiritual understanding. His first anointing took place when he was chosen by God out of the company of his brothers. Like David, the Lord does not choose an individual and offer them a special anointing without gifting them with the gifts needed to accomplish His purpose, both in them and through their lives.

Young David was not presented initially to the prophet Samuel. His father had presented his seven brothers. Jesse started with the eldest to the youngest. Each time the prophet Samuel said that none of the brothers was the one God wanted to lead His people. David wasn't considered, there, or aware of what was going on. It was Samuel (who had spiritual understanding) who asked if there was another son available to be presented. Jesse's reaction tells us that he did not consider David due to his age.

Once David was summoned and presented, led by the Holy Spirit, Samuel took in his hand a horn of oil. That horn had been taken off an animal. It probably was a ram's horn. Then, the horn was filled with anointing oil (Exodus 30:22–25). The oil was poured upon the top of David's head. The poured oil *ran down from his head.* As the oil ran over the surface of his body, the spices excited his senses and the senses of those around him. Everyone in the room knew something special was taking place. David was no longer to be seen as just a young shepherd boy or as their little brother. He was chosen by God in a special way for the purpose of leading God's people. It was the initiation of the Spirit. It was a moment in time that David could look back to. (A type of Jesus being anointed in the womb and leaping when Elizabeth prophesied to Mary.)

Many of us, including me in 1974, have had a similar experience. I'm sure that moment stands out in your memory, just as it did in David's and mine.

On the day that David was chosen, so were his sons that would reign upon Israel's throne. His seed was chosen. This includes Solomon, Rehoboam, his great-grandsons, and so on, all the way to Christ Jesus (see Matthew 1:1). The Lord Jesus Christ, the son of David, the son of Abraham, was anointed and chosen. Now we who are *in Him have also been chosen, as well!*

We have been chosen to be like Him, to hear His voice, to minister in His Name, and to reign with Him. The day God anointed David, He was reaching down through time to even you! You were chosen, and now, because of your acceptance of Christ as your Savior and Lord, you have an anointing within you (1 John 2:27). The anointed one, and His anointing, lives in you. His anointing is working to change you and expose to you the mysteries of God because His anointing is within you!

> *We have been chosen to be like Him, to hear His voice, to minister in His Name, and to reign with Him.*

Our wonderful heavenly Father desires for you to be filled with knowledge and understanding. Like David, you were called and chosen from your mother's womb (read Isaiah 49). From before the very first moment of your life, you were called and chosen to be in Christ and to have knowledge and understanding concerning the mysteries of God.

Several years after the first anointing, a second anointing took place in David's life. In 2 Samuel 2:4 (NIV), it says, "The men of Judah came to Hebron, and there they anointed David king over the tribe of Judah." It's important to note the second anointing uses the Hebrew word *meshack*. It is different from the one used in 1 Samuel 17. This word means to smear with oil or ointment.[66]

A second level of knowledge and understanding takes place when we are consecrated to the work God has given for us to do. Beyond exciting the senses, this level of His anointing occurs when the hand of God fully encounters our lives. In my book, *Gifts of the Ascended Christ*, I speak to the hand of God being the complete five-fold ministry. There comes a time when those around us take notice and see His touch on our lives. Our appearance changes. Our ministry changes. Soon others begin to see something in us that stands out. It is no longer about what has been poured on us but that which is being rubbed or smeared on us. It is usually accompanied when ministry gifts (five-fold— apostle, prophet, evangelist, pastor, and teacher) lay hands on us and ask God to ordain us to the ministry. This is generally followed by a time of difficulty that causes us to rely upon who and what we know to be true. This occurred in my life in 1980.

Dr. Paul Lowenberg had been asked to preach and minister in my ordination service. That night he preached from John's Gospel. John 12:21 (NIV) says, "They came to Philip, who was from Bethsaida in Galilee, with a request. 'Sir,' they said, 'we would like to see Jesus.'"

Dr. Lowenberg's message was basically this: When people see us, they should see Jesus. He spoke about the way Jesus prayed. About the way Jesus preached. And about the purpose of Jesus, who came to *save that which was lost*. That night when he, my pastor, and others (the hand of God) laid hands on me, the power of the Holy Spirit not only filled the auditorium in an awesome and glorious manner, but my life was changed in a dramatic way.

Let me try to explain. If I would take your hand today and just pour a little bit of oil on your hand and then ask you to shake the oil off or take a towel and wipe it away. You would still be able to smell that the oil had been there. The aroma or scent of the oil would still reach your senses. But then, in a few minutes, or at least a few hours, after the oil dried and disappeared, what would be left? A memory. In fact, after three days, you wouldn't even be able to tell that I ever poured oil on your hand. But if I would take that same oil and smear it on your hand, your wrist, and up your arm, then the other arm, your face, and head. Something different would happen. The skin on your hand, wrist, and arm would be changed by the emollient in the oil. Yes, the scent of the oil would dissipate, but the work of the oil would last for days. And if it was repeated several more times? Over time, your skin would become softer, more pliable, and more moist.

Sadly, many modern Christians have never realized the anointing has been poured upon their lives, except for their memory of coming to Christ. The doctrine of the *laying of hands* has either been forgotten or ignored in most churches. Then there are those who do lay hands on people but do not spend the time needed in the Presence of the Lord and to effectively give what they have been given. Because they do not value spiritual knowledge, understanding, and wisdom, any ordination service of such may create an emotional response, but over time it will not equate to real spiritual value. Reliance on the traditions of men has usurped the anointed manifestation of the Presence of God. Yes, these folks have come to Christ and have everlasting life. Yes, they have believed and called upon the Name of Jesus.

They can remember that momentary flash when God saved them and made them ready to go to heaven.

Yet, there is a difference between God's anointing being placed within one at salvation and the anointing being smeared onto one's life. It is important that any prophetic ministry have the touch of God on the ministry and on their life! *One is visitation; the other is habitation!*

For when the touch of God is on your life, your appearance changes. You are being moved into present truth by the Spirit as He leads you from faith to faith and from glory to glory.

And like Jesus, David was anointed a third time. His third anointing took place in 2 Samuel 5. I have adapted the description of the anointing from Fausset's Bible Dictionary and really appreciate what He says about the word *anoint.*

> *The sacred use of oil was for consecrating things or persons to God. The oil is a symbol of the Holy Spirit, and as applied to things gave them a ceremonial sacredness, fitting them for holy ministrations. As applied to prophets (1 Chronicles 16:22; 1 Kings 19:16), priests (Leviticus 4:3), and kings (Isaiah 45:1), it marked their* consecration to their calling and office, and was a symbol of the spiritual qualification divinely imparted for its due discharge *(see Exodus 30:29–30). David's second anointing is a type of Jesus being anointed at His baptism when the Holy Spirit landed upon Him. The Lord's third anointing took place in the house of Lazarus by Mary (John 12:1–3).*[67]

David was anointed three times. First to the right of kingship, then anointed king over Judah, then anointed king over the whole nation of Israel. Jesus the Messiah was twice so designated in the Old Testament (Psalm 2:2; Daniel 9:25–26), as prophet, priest, and king. He is the center of all prophecy, the antitype of all priesthood, and the source and end of all kingship (Luke 4:18; Acts 4:27; 10:38). Jesus was anointed with the Holy Spirit first from the womb, then at His baptism (John 1:32–33, 41) and then for His burial (John 12:3).

> *Hereby the New Testament marks Him as the Messiah of the Old Testament (Acts 9:22; 17:2–3; 18:5, 28.) What He is His people are, Messiahs or "anointed ones" by union with Him (Zec. 4:14), having the unction of the Holy Spirit. (2 Corinthians 1:21; 1 John 2:20).*[68]

All the elders of Israel came to Hebron, and King David made a league with them. He was then brought before the Lord, and they anointed David as king over Israel. In this anointing, these elders were of the whole nation. David's first anointing was about *being chosen for something.* His second was *for his empowerment to accomplish what he had been chosen to do.* The third had to do *with who David was to become. He was more than a king, more than the king of Judah, but now David was king of the nation!*

Do you see how that relates to the Lord Jesus? Anointed and chosen before birth (from the foundation of the world); anointed a second time at His baptism by His Father (to accomplish His ministry—see Isaiah 61); and finally anointed for His burial in John 12 when Mary rubbed the oil into His feet with her hair. Looking forward to this moment, the prophet Isaiah said, "How beautiful on the mountains are the feet of those who bring good news, who proclaim peace, who bring good tidings, who proclaim salvation, who say to Zion, 'Your God reigns!'" (Isaiah 52:7, NIV). Just after His last anointing, Jesus declared openly to His disciples that He would die for the sins of the world, be buried, and be resurrected as Savior, Messiah, and Lord! Hallelujah!

When the anointing is rubbed into our lives, we take on the elements of His (Christ's) anointing. As His anointed ones, our spiritual lives are no longer about what we experience or what we do but who we are and become. We are now crucified with Christ, and the life we live is His life! (Galatians 2:20) Again, most contemporary Christians have settled for only the first anointing. Why? Experiencing the supernatural is exciting. It doesn't cost much because someone else paid the price. One usually doesn't have to do anything. It does not require the commitment needed to live a life full of the Holy Spirit's power and Presence. Then, they go from special service to special service seeking to find someone else to *pour oil on them.*

We are standing on the precipice of a great prophetic shift. Thankfully there are many who are sensing a new clarion call. Like the prophetess Anna, they have been waiting for the appearance of Christ in a dimension they have not known here to fore. The earth is calling out for the manifestation of mature sons of God! Such maturity comes as one is taught and trained by the Spirit. In this hour, we must be willing to spend time in His Presence, seeking to have His anointing smeared upon and rubbed into our lives. Yes, it will cost more from us. But the price is worth it. For with each deep experience in God, the anointing becomes even more precious to our lives and ministry.

We will need to be willing to be like Paul and forget every-thing that is behind us (both bad and good, both before we were saved and after). Our hearts must be turned fully and completely toward God. We must seek Him with a whole heart and enter the press (as Paul put it in 2 Corinthians 1:8). The coming deluge of the Spirit will require preparation, passion, and pressure. This new spiritual dimension in Christ will involve Him taking prece-dence in your life, followed by perseverance and patience.

I want you just to examine your own heart. How many times have you bailed out of the process? Do you know what it cost you?

How many times have you tried to share your understanding of Christ without being prepared? What did it cost you? How many times have you given up when the pressure became heavy? And someone told you it wasn't worth it.

What did it cost you?

I pray that you will choose the treasures of Christ Jesus. I pray you are beginning to seek to have the anointing *rubbed into your life*. Ask the Holy Spirit to help you have divine knowledge, wisdom, and understanding. See yourself as His anointed. Such revelation will bring about magnificent change in your life. Life will no longer be about what you have or what you do. Your life will take on the will, ways, and wonders of Christ Jesus because you will see yourself *in Him!* Hallelujah!

CHAPTER SIXTEEN:

God's Secret Wisdom

No, we declare God's secret wisdom, a mystery that has been hidden and that God destined for our glory before time began. None of the rulers of this age understood it, for if they had, they would not have crucified the Lord of glory.

— 1 Corinthians 2:7–8 (NIV)

According to Paul's letter to the Corinthians, God's secret wisdom is hidden in a mystery (*theou sophian en mustêriôi*). And because it's hidden, it cannot be comprehended with natural wisdom. There are things that God has prepared for those that love Him. Wonderful things. Glorious things. Spiritual things. These prepared things can only be spiritually discerned, known, understood, spoken, and accomplished. Such wisdom can only be revealed in Christ because in Him are hidden all the treasures of wisdom and knowledge.

My goal is that they may be encouraged in heart and united in love, so that they may have the full riches of complete understanding, in order that they may

know the mystery of God, namely, Christ, in whom are
hidden all the treasures of wisdom and knowledge.

— Colossians 2:2–3 (NIV)

Christ is "the mystery of God." The treasures of His knowledge and wisdom are no longer hidden. They are now to be fully comprehended as we offer ourselves to God as living sacrifices, who have become both open and receptive to such things. Because they are found in Christ, fresh wisdom comes through repeated discovery and can be known in the fullness of our capacity.

But to those whom God has called, both Jews and
Greeks, Christ the power of God and the wisdom of
God.

— 1 Corinthians 1:24 (NIV)

It is because of him that you are in Christ Jesus, who
has become for us wisdom from God.

— 1 Corinthians 1:30 (NIV)

Joshua was a person filled with the spirit of wisdom. Deuteronomy 34:9 (NIV) says, "Now Joshua son of Nun was filled with the spirit of wisdom because Moses had laid his hands on him." The spirit of wisdom that filled Joshua that day did not simply happen or transpire out of the blue. The wisdom of God was a result of Joshua's commitment and devotion. It is believed Joshua was born sometime after Moses first left Egypt and fled to Midian in the Arabian Desert. Joshua was born a slave, lived in the Land of Goshen, and came to serve as Moses' assistant for forty years. Soon after crossing the Red Sea with Moses, Joshua was chosen to lead a band of Israelite men against the Amalekites (Exodus 17). Along with eleven others, he also led the Israelite spies into the promised land for the purpose of bringing back a report (Numbers 14). Upon his return, only Caleb agreed with Joshua saying, "We are able to go up and take the country." Due to the fear and negative report of the other ten spies, the Israelite nation spent forty years wandering in the desert. During that time, Joshua served Moses. Apparently, Moses discerned (by the Spirit) his heart for God and cultivated Joshua's sterling qualities. Joshua learned to lead by obeying first; then, he ruled for God, not himself.[69]

Joshua was chosen by God to lead Israel out of a slave mentality (which had developed over 400 years) into the land of promise. Can you imagine the responsibility he must have felt? He was chosen to follow in the footsteps of the great Moses, who was a prophet like no other (see Deuteronomy 34:10). For forty years, the nation of Israel had been led by a man who, at times, had stood face-to-face with the God of the universe. Moses was able to accomplish some astonishing things, such as, by raising his shepherd's rod, the Red Sea parted, and God made a highway of escape on dry ground. Then he used that same stick to cause water to gush from a rock. Along with several other miracles at the hand of Moses, there were many times, after he had spoken to God, Moses' face literally glowed like a light bulb with the glory of God.

Following Moses' death, it was Joshua's turn to lead Israel. God made a promise to Joshua, "As I was with Moses, so I will be with you; I will never leave you nor forsake you" (Joshua 1:5, NIV). But even then, Joshua needed the spiritual wisdom that had been imparted to him at the hands of Moses. Unlike Moses, who had led the nation with individual displays of power and authority, Joshua was given instructions by the Lord to use a more *team-oriented approach*. When crossing the Jordan, the Lord told him that he was to have four priests to carry the ark of the covenant into the flooding river. There is little doubt that many of the Israelite people believed Joshua to be foolish or silly.

But Joshua pressed forward undaunted by criticism or fear. The spiritual wisdom we learn from Israel crossing the Jordan and entering the promised land almost defies description. First, there were four priests. The number four is the biblical number of *creation*. (For on the fourth day of the *creation week*, God completed the material universe.) Second, instead of leading individually as Moses had done, Joshua was given instructions to have the priests take the lead. The priests, who had been called and chosen by God to minister to Him and His people, were to carry the ark (a type of Jesus) high and lifted up on their shoulders, above all of Israel. And remember, four plus one equals five, the biblical number of grace! Together with the ark, they were instructed to step into the Jordan at flood stage, going before the people into that which had been promised to their father, Abraham.

When the four priests (a type of Jesus, the Son of Man) and the ark of the covenant (a type of Christ, the Son of God) was carried upon their shoulders (lifted up on the cross of Calvary) stepped into the Jordan River (a type of death), the waters parted all the way northward from the town of Adam (a type of the first fallen man—named Adam) all the way to the Dead Sea (a type of the last death). The Israelite people entered as one people, not two by two or ten by ten, but as one people (both Jew and Gentile, male and female, slave and free) into the promised land (not only a land of promise but a life of promise) and the home to every believer's spiritual father, Abraham. God had opened a new and living way! He had opened a portal into a dimension of victory and prosperity!

From that day, Joshua led Israel in a much different way than Moses had done. It was all due to the spiritual wisdom imparted to him. In fact, several months later, the Bible says that Joshua was given a day like none other.

> On the day the LORD gave the Amorites over to Israel, Joshua said to the LORD in the presence of Israel: "Sun, stand still over Gibeon, and you, moon, over the Valley of Aijalon." So the sun stood still, and the moon stopped, till the nation avenged itself on its enemies, as it is written in the Book of Jashar. *The sun stopped in the middle of the sky and delayed going down about a full day.* There has never been a day like it before or since, a day when the LORD listened to a human being. Surely the LORD was fighting for Israel!
>
> — Joshua 10:12–14 (NIV)
> (emphasis added by the author)

Great spiritual wisdom accompanied Joshua until the day of his death. He was given spiritual understanding when it came to conquering the cities of the Ammonites, Canaanites, and the other people who had moved into the land while Israel was in Egypt for over four hundred years. Joshua was also given special wisdom to root out the secret sin of Achan and overcome all the hindrances that were set before him.

There are several others in the Old Testament who were given the special impartation of God's glorious wisdom. Men like Solomon, Elisha, and Daniel, as well as women like Ruth and Esther, give us a glimpse into the manifestation of God's supernatural wisdom.

There isn't any doubt that the glorious wisdom of God flowed most out of the life of our Lord and Savior, Jesus Christ. His words, His actions, and His life overflowed with boundless wisdom to the point that God revealed to Paul that "Christ is power and the wisdom of God" (1 Corinthians 1:24).

The hidden treasures of God's wisdom and knowledge (Colossians 2:2–30) were fully manifested in Jesus Christ. He came to Earth—God in the form of man. He humbled Himself, taking the form of a servant, and was made in the likeness of men. And, yet, through the anointing (the power of the Spirit) upon Him, He healed the sick, raised the dead, and set captives free. He freely shared with His disciples the treasures of wisdom for the purpose of enriching their understanding of Himself and the will of the Father. He revealed the unsearchable glories of heaven and illuminated those closest to Him to the mysteries of God, especially Peter, James, and John. He unveiled to them the secrets of the kingdom so they would have an abundance of understanding (Matthew 13:11).

Several Hebrew words are translated as *wisdom* in the Old Testament. But in the New Testament and especially in the writings of the apostle Paul, wisdom came from his use of the Greek word *sophia*. Paul took the word first used by the Greek philosophers hundreds of years earlier to describe the highest form of wisdom, *spiritual wisdom*.

What role in the future will spiritual wisdom play? I believe it will call us toward, as Ellis put it, "gifts of inspired speech and discernment." Such gifts were associated with the prophets and wise men of the Old Testament and Qumran.[70] Such wisdom executed by Paul's associates resembles the pesher-type interpretation in the Dead Sea Scrolls. Pesher interpretation occurs when a scriptural passage is followed by a spiritual interpretation that can generally be classified as "actualizing" or eschatological in nature. It has increasingly been recognized as having been divinely revealed in some manner.[71]

> *Pesher interpretation occurs when a scriptural passage is followed by a spiritual interpretation.*

George Brooke notes that such interpretive material is not presented as "secondary or derivative but as coherent with the divine communication received by the prophet." In other words, the interpretations of God's secret wisdom contained in the *pesharim* are divinely given, authoritative, and on the level of the words of the original prophet. The authors of the *pesharim* apparently believed that the fulfillment of the "mysteries" contained in the writings of the prophets of old had been revealed by God to them and that the events that the prophets foretold had been, or would be, realized in the authors' own time.[72]

Such spiritual wisdom proceeds to give us present truth as to the divine nature of Christ and the dynamic ministry of the Holy Spirit. It is acquired by revelation and requires acute spiritual devotion and experience. It usually includes spiritual illumination of, first, who we are in Christ (sons, not servants); second, we have received and are receiving inheritance, not wages; third, divine order and representation cannot be overlooked; and finally, we must search the Scriptures for in them we come to understand the "present truth" of God. This includes having discretion concerning the impartation of Christian truth and should result in the knowledge, understanding, and practice of God's wisdom for godly and upright living.

Such was lost to mankind in the fall of Adam. Only at intermittent times was such spiritual wisdom given to individuals in the Old Testament. But Jesus came to redeem and restore all that had been lost by Adam. He said, "For the Son of Man came to seek and to save the lost" (Luke 19:10, NIV). The King James Version uses the term, *that which was lost*. Please notice that Jesus did not use the word "who" but rather "what." He then continued with a parable because He was near Jerusalem, and the people thought that the kingdom of God was going to appear (Luke 9:11–26). What made the people think that the kingdom of God was about to appear? Apparently, the very special wisdom Jesus conveyed that day. It had to be something other than Jesus calling Zacchaeus from the tree and telling everyone that the tax collector and publican was considered by Jesus *a son of Abraham*.

The words of Jesus, "of seeking and saving that which was lost," are in stark contrast to what most organized Christianity has been focused on for the past five hundred years. The organized church at large has been focused on saving those who are lost (the unredeemed of mankind) and should be. But the words of Jesus mentioned in this instance declare He came to save *what was lost*. Jesus fully understood that mankind had lost the treasures of heaven (beginning with a relationship with God), which specifically includes the spiritual knowledge, understanding, and wisdom that God had given in His original purpose and plan for His creation to Adam.

As I said before, God's original purpose from the beginning was to establish a family of sons and daughters, not servants. Servants have little real relationship with their master other than providing service. They receive wages and have no inheritance. In contrast, we are sons of God. We are heirs and joint heirs with Jesus Christ. We are a commonwealth of citizens, not members of a religious order. We are redeemed. God has chosen in His marvelous wisdom to extend His heavenly government out of heaven and pour His influence into the earth through us (salt and light). We are no longer citizens of the earth. We are citizens of heaven who live on the earth. We are citizens of His commonwealth; altogether, we have His great spiritual wealth in common (Romans 8:17; Ephesians 2:12; 1 Peter 3:7).

God's original purpose from the beginning was to establish a family of sons and daughters, not servants.

Acts 16 is the backdrop to the book of Philippians. Paul had been born a Roman citizen, and Philippi was a colony in the Roman province of Macedonia. The apostle used the Greek word *politeuma* in Philippians 3:20–21 (NIV),

> *But our citizenship* [politeuma] *is in heaven. And we eagerly await a Savior from there, the Lord Jesus Christ, who, by the power that enables him to bring everything under his control, will transform our lowly bodies so that they will be like his glorious body.*

He did so to show us that our manner of life should come from heavenly places. It is from that posture that we "look for our Savior." For the law of the Spirit of life in Christ Jesus has made us free from the law of sin and death (Romans 8:2). Our citizenry, all our rights, and privileges, are in heaven. This ascended life is the higher life. We cannot behave as citizens of heaven until we see what God sees, how God sees, and when God sees. We must regulate and conduct our lives according to the "royal law," the "law of liberty."[73]

Adam had not only lost his intimate relationship with God, but he also lost the ability to share in the supernatural wisdom that God used to establish His colony of heaven on Earth. The intermittent wisdom conveyed through Moses, Joshua, Esther, Solomon, Daniel, and others could not reveal the depth of hidden treasures of wisdom and knowledge. Such can only be fully understood by being *in Christ* and by the unfolding revelation given by the Holy Spirit. In the book, *The Pneumatics and the Early Christian Mission*, Ellis again speaks of how the Holy Spirit or spirits (angels) have a special relation to *the wise*. This endowment gives "knowledge in the mysteries of God's wisdom and the angelic spirits of knowledge in the heavenly council of God."[74]

Some will take this to mean that God is *spooky*. I do not believe that is such the case. Jesus wants us to know and execute His heavenly treasures and, in doing so, be *laying up treasures in heaven*. He did not teach that the kingdom of heaven was *eerie* or *scary*, but within that kingdom is a spiritual and revelational knowledge, understanding, and wisdom that would attract people to the message and salvation of Jesus Christ. Many a Pentecostal and Charismatic person has tried to be *mysteriously spooky and strange* about the things of God, making their insight impractical and, for the most part, rejected by others. This has caused their ministries to be either misunderstood, unacceptable, or ineffective. God has not called us to be impractical people. The glorious treasures of heaven are not so. Neither are the treasures that we will see exhibited in the coming prophetic shift. In the coming chapters, I will offer you what I believe are the first steps to a spiritual process that will enable you to fully embrace the upcoming downpour of the Spirit and prophetic ministry.

CHAPTER SEVENTEEN:

Spiritual Gifts (Part One)

Now about the gifts of the Spirit, brothers and sisters, I do not want you to be uninformed.

— 1 Corinthians 12:1 (NIV)

"When he ascended on high, he took many captives and gave gifts to his people." ...So Christ himself gave the apostles, the prophets, the evangelists, the pastors and teachers.

— Ephesians 4:8, 11 (NIV)

The word translated for spiritual "gifts" in Ephesians 4:8 comes from the Greek word *doma*. *Doma* simply means a *gift*.[75] It is from the Greek root *didomi*, which means:

1. To give.
2. To give something to someone.
   a. Of one's own accord to give one something, to the advantage of the person receiving the gift.

2. To give to another for the purpose of supplying, furnishing, or providing the necessary for their needs.[76]

These are gifts *Christ gave to His church*. All these gifts can be found in only one man, the Lord Jesus Christ. Having qualified them to be demonstrated on the earth through His ministry, He gave these gifts to the church at His resurrection (Ephesians 4:8). He also gave them for the purpose of furnishing or supplying His church with the necessary ministries to enable His people to *grow up in Him*. He gave them these gifts…

> *To equip his people for works of service, so that the body of Christ may be built up, until we all reach unity in the faith and in the knowledge of the Son of God and become mature, attaining to the whole measure of the fullness of Christ. Then we will no longer be infants, tossed back and forth by the waves, and blown here and there by every wind of teaching and by the cunning and craftiness of people in their deceitful scheming. Instead, speaking the truth in love, we will grow to become in every respect the mature body of him who is the head, that is, Christ.*
>
> — Ephesians 4:12–15 (NIV)

Without these gifts, the church cannot become what God intended it to be, namely, His vehicle to bring people into the fullness of seeing heaven on Earth. These gifts include the apostle, prophet, evangelist, pastor, and teacher. When I wrote about these gifts in my book, *Gifts from the Ascended Christ*, I gave the illustration that these five gifts (God's number of grace) working together are likened unto the human hand. Each gift, like each finger, plays an important part in completing God's purpose in creating the human hand. The apostle, like the thumb, is separate from the others and has a dimension of strength the other fingers do not have. The prophet is likened to the finger we generally point or lead with. The middle finger represents the evangelist whom God uses to reach with. The ring finger is associated with the pastor, who watches over God's covenant with His people, and the teacher (the little finger) brings balance to the hand. Each is vitally important. If you don't think so, try to grip something without using your thumb, point at something, or reach. I won't take the time to rehearse the complete understanding the Holy Spirit gave to me concerning these gifts. If you would like more information about them, you can order *The Gifts of the Ascended Christ* from our ministry online or at any Christian bookstore.

The second group of gifts I want to address comes from the Greek word *charisma*. *Charisma*, used in the context of Romans 12, literally means "a grace."[77] *The graces listed in Romans 12 are the gifts or graces Christ put* in His church *for the purpose of service.* They are different than the gifts listed in Ephesians and serve a different purpose. These gifts were not given to the church to bring about maturity and unity, but rather they are "the result of grace." (This comes from the suffix *ma* being added to the Greek word *charis*.) Every Christian, irrespective of spiritual standing, whether carnal or spiritual, immature or mature, has God's indwelling grace within them. And His grace has the potential of demonstrating one of these "graces" or "grace gifts." Paul said,

*Just as each of us has one body with many members,
and these members do not all have the same function, so in Christ we, though many, form one body,
and each member belongs to all the others. We have
different gifts, according to the grace given to each of
us. If your gift is prophesying, then prophesy in accor-
dance with your faith; if it is serving, then serve; if it
is teaching, then teach; if it is to encourage, then give
encouragement; if it is giving, then give generously; if
it is to lead, do it diligently; if it is to show mercy, do it
cheerfully.*

— Romans 12:4–8 (NIV)

The demonstration of these gifts or graces is activated not
by the Holy Spirit but by the individual. Yes, God is the giver
and sustainer of all grace and these gifts. But it is to be observed
that the apostle here assumes that every Christian possesses, in
some form, not only the marvelous grace of God, which has been
bestowed and continues to distribute these graces, but Paul sees
a believing soul without the manifestation of these grace gifts, is
a monstrosity. No believer is without grace. No believer is void,
therefore, of one or more of these graces and, therefore, cannot
say they are without some duties.[78] This list is not exhaustive nor
logically arranged. Maclaren states there is a certain loose order
that may be noted here, which may be profitable for us to trace.
They are in number seven—the sacred number; and are capable
of being divided, as so many of the series of sevens are, into two
portions, one containing four and the other three. The former
includes more public works, to each of which a person might
be specially devoted as their life work for and in the church.

Three are more private and may be conceived to have a wider relation to the world.[79] It should be noted that, in most instances, these gracious gifts are associated with our personality, talents, and abilities. Each gift can reach its ultimate manifestation in the Christian who has presented themselves as a living sacrifice (Romans 12:1–2) and accepts the responsibility to serve others.

Paul states if a man's gift is prophesying, let him use it in proportion to his faith. And so, it is with the remainder of the list. Each gift works by faith. If we are led to serve, we should seek the faith to serve. If we are compelled to teach, then by faith, we find a place to teach and develop teaching skills. If it is encouragement, look for an opportunity in every day and every place to encourage. And the same should be done if you believe your gift is giving, leadership, or the showing of mercy. Find a place to serve and serve!

For more information on the gifts listed in Romans 12, I encourage you to read, *True Spirituality: Becoming a Romans 12 Christian* and *Living on the Edge: Dare to Experience True Spirituality* by Chip Ingram.

CHAPTER EIGHTEEN:

Spiritual Gifts (Part Two)

Now concerning spiritual gifts.

— 1 Corinthians 12:1 (KJV)

The phrase *spiritual gifts* in 1 Corinthians 12:1 is actually better translated as "spirituals" and is revealed in the Greek word *pneumatikos*.[80] These are gifts *Christ gave for the betterment and ministry of His church*. The *pneumatikos* are gifts that generally work through *pneumatics*. Remember, they were early Christians who were characterized by spiritual gifts of inspired speech, divine discernment, and spiritual understanding. The *pneumatikos* are not permanent acquisitions or talents like the gifts listed in Romans 12. Neither are they permanent gifts given as those in Ephesians 4. These gifts are instantaneous enablements by the Holy Spirit *because these gifts are His gifts*. He has chosen to manifest them (the word manifest is *phaneroo*, which means to make visible or known what has been hidden or unknown) and administrate them (*diakonos*, meaning to execute the commands or wishes of another). These gifts include the power to know, say, or do something beyond a person's natural ability for the purpose of fulfilling a specific purpose of God *at the moment* the Holy Spirit decides to work through that individual.

Even among Pentecostals and Charismatic congregations, the manifestation and administration of these spiritual gifts or "*pnuematikos charismata*" have waned dramatically over the past twenty or so years. But it is these spiritual gifts that are needed most when God's people are facing difficult times or situations (like we are now and even more so in the future). In times when we need an answer to a problem, wisdom in a certain situation, or the faith to overcome an attack from the enemy, these gifts will manifest through a person by the Holy Spirit *as He enables them*. Each of the gifts is a supernatural manifestation of the Holy Spirit's ministry through the believer *as a result of God's grace*.

Each gift of the Spirit is active in strength, expression, and performance.

These gifts have varieties (differences) of working, endowment, enablement, service, and effectiveness. Each gift of the Spirit is active in strength, expression, and performance.

The spiritual gifts in 1 Corinthians 12 have three different purposes. They were given to edify (*oikodome*), which means the act of building up, strengthening, and reinforcing; to exhort (*paraklesis*), which means to encourage, counsel, and advise; and to comfort (*paramuthia*), which means to care for, show empathy, remove sadness, and encourage others.

As a rule, the inspired speaking gifts (tongues, interpretation of tongues, and prophecy) are generally evidenced and delivered in glorious and poetical language. There are times in which the gift assumes a certain rhythmical character but is not bound to a narrow and mechanical meter. The individual peculiarities of a person through whom the Holy Spirit is manifesting one of these spiritual gifts enter its form and manifestation. To one person, the Holy Spirit will lend a "knowing" or preponderance of a coming manifestation; but another person may have no preponderance at all.

> *What then shall we say, brothers and sisters? When you come together, each of you has a hymn, or a word of instruction, a revelation, a tongue or an interpretation. Everything must be done so that the church may be built up.*
>
> — 1 Corinthians 14:26 (NIV)

The second set of gifts mentioned by Paul provides supernatural knowledge, understanding, discernment, or wisdom. These gifts include the "discerning of spirits," which is different than typical discernment. Typical discernment is the act or process of exhibiting keen insight and good judgment. On the other hand, the *discerning of spirits* is generally manifested as divine understanding concerning the source of words or actions. Such can be human, demonic, angelic, or the Holy Spirit. The gift of the word of knowledge (*logos gnosis*)[81] provides knowledge or understanding that is deeper and a more perfect knowledge of spiritual truth.

Where personal knowledge comes by acquaintance with facts, truths, or principles, as from study or investigation, the word of knowledge comes by the revelation of facts, events, or principles outside the realm of personal knowledge. Such knowledge can only be explained by the Spirit's knowledge being conveyed in and through a willing and open individual. This gift works when the Spirit illuminates biblical truth as it relates to types, shadows, and examples. This gift works at times to enable a person to function as a teacher of supernatural truth.

The gift may also give one the ability to minister to the "past hurts or experiences" of another by revealing into the mind of the person being used a past fact that is unknown to them. It may also provide the ability to determine the "present truth" in a section of time or opportunity to minister to a person's need.

The gift of the word of wisdom (*logos sophia*)[82] speaks to the wisdom of God as evidenced in forming and executing His counsels among the Godhead during the formation and government of the world and the Scriptures. The word of wisdom can only be effectively shared in a mind that is being transformed by the renewing of the Spirit and the washing of the Word of God (Romans 12:2, Ephesians 5:26). Its administration is concerned with the revelation that provides facts or counsel for the future. This gift may provide divine knowledge to the mysteries of God and thus enable prophetic ministers to reveal the "coming move" of the Spirit as well as the ability to minister to the "future hurts" of another person or group of people.

All speaking and knowing gifts should bring one or more of the following: edification (the building up of a person or a group of people as a whole), comfort (hope, encouragement, faith), consolation (cheer and joy), revelation (disclosure of spiritual mysteries or to reveal direction for a person or church), special knowledge, understanding, or wisdom that affirms the Bible as well as aspects of the Bible that are held as truth. Remember, God works through different people differently! There are differences in the administration of these gifts as they are ministered through different people who have different personalities and talents.

Finally, there are power working gifts. The first is the gift of faith (*pnuematikos charismata pistis*). This is not the faith of surrender or saving faith, but wonderworking, miracle-believing faith like that seen in Matthew 17:20; 21:21. Simply put, it is the faith to believe God for the extraordinary.

> *This went on for two years, so that all the Jews and Greeks who lived in the province of Asia heard the word of the Lord.* God did extraordinary *miracles through Paul, so that even handkerchiefs and aprons that had touched him were taken to the sick, and their illnesses were cured and the evil spirits left them.*
>
> — Acts 19:10–12 (NIV)
> (emphasis added by the author)

Included in Paul's list are the gifts of healing (*charismata iamatôn*). This gift is from the Greek word *Iama*, which is an old word from *iaomai* and can be found only in Paul's first letter to the Corinthians.[83] It means "acts of healing," as in Acts 4:30 as well as James 5:14 (of elders) and Luke 7:21 (of Jesus). Examples of the manifestation of this gift are seen in Naaman (2 Kings 5) and the woman with the issue of blood (Mark 5). In most instances, there appears to be a special manifested grace to the person receiving the ministry. Healing may not take place immediately, as with the lepers in Luke 17:12, and may be progressive, as happened with the blind man in John 9.

The gift of workings of miraculous powers (*energêmata dunameôn*) is demonstrated at times as "signs" (*semeia*), which are generally a mark by which persons or things are distinguished and made known. This gift usually addresses the spiritual senses for the purpose of displaying the existence of supersensible and, therefore, divine power.[84] Thus, the plagues of Egypt were "signs" of divine displeasure against the Egyptians (Exodus 4:8; Joshua 24:17), and the miracles of Jesus were "signs" to attest His unique relationship with God (Matthew 12:38; John 2:18; Acts 2:22). These miracles can also be wonders (*terata*).

In the New Testament, the ordinary Greek verb for wonder is *thaumazo*, but the most frequent Greek noun used in Scripture is *terata*, which means a "marvel" or "portent." The Hebrew word is *pala'*. In both Testaments, a "wonder" is chiefly a miraculous work, so in the Gospels, the feeling of wonder is chiefly drawn out by the marvelous displays of Christ's power and wisdom (Matthew 15:31; Mark 6:51; Luke 4:22, etc.).[85]

This gift can also be manifested as "powers" (*dunameis*). These are the "mighty works" of God. They are denoted by the term "powers" in Matthew 11:21–23; see the Revised Version margin. These deeds alter nature in some way, like Jesus walking on water or calming the sea. There are three specific "seasons" of miracles listed in the Bible, the miracles associated with Moses and Joshua, Elijah and Elisha, and Jesus, including His ministry in and through the first-century apostles.

Preparing for the coming outpouring of the Spirit includes our receiving understanding of the ministry and administration of these gifts. These spiritual gifts will only be effective out of a heart of love, a transformed mind, a grateful attitude, and a life that is balanced with both humility and confidence. Such a life is enabled to encounter, embrace, and then enjoy the marvelous treasures of heaven. Living such a life embraces progressive spiritual understanding and the willingness to continue in the revelation of spiritual things.

But the word of the LORD was unto them precept upon precept, precept upon precept; line upon line, line upon line; here a little, and there a little; that they might go, and fall backward, and be broken, and snared, and taken.

— Isaiah 28:13 (KJV)

They go from strength to strength, every one of them in Zion appeareth before God.

— Psalm 84:7 (KJV)

God's Word and Spirit must always be proceeding into and through our lives. None of us should confine ourselves to spiritual life without the development of both heart and mind, attitude and actions, as well as ministry and service. We must not limit the operation or administration of the Holy Spirit in any dimension. We are admonished to grow in the grace and knowledge of the Son of God. We are to speak the truth in love, so we will in all things grow up into Him, who is the head, that is, Christ. We are instructed to integrate the mysteries which the Holy Spirit reveals to us until we all reach unity in the faith and in the knowledge of the Son of God and become mature (Ephesians 4:11–16).

Prevailing prayer must also be involved. J. Stuart Holden said,

Here is the secret of prevailing prayer, to pray under a direct inspiration of the Holy Spirit, whose petitions for

us and through us are always according to the Divine purpose, and hence certain of answer.

Praying in the Holy Spirit each day brings us into cooperation with the will of God, and such prayer is always victorious (see Ephesians 6:18–21). The secret of a dynamic prayer life is "be filled with the Spirit," who is "the Spirit of grace and supplication." Romans 8:11 (KJV) tells us, "But if the Spirit of him that raised up Jesus from the dead dwell in you, he that raised up Christ from the dead shall also quicken your mortal bodies by his Spirit that dwelleth in you." In other words, there are no heavenly treasures given that have not been made available to every believer and follower of Christ Jesus. Peter listed the treasures needed for living such a life in 2 Peter 1:3–8 (NIV),

> *There are no heavenly treasures given that have not been made available to every believer and follower of Christ Jesus.*

> *His divine power has given us everything we need for a godly life through our knowledge of him who called us by his own glory and goodness. Through these he has given us his very great and precious promises, so that through them you may participate in the divine nature, having escaped the corruption in the world caused by evil desires. For this very reason, make every effort to add to your faith goodness; and to goodness, knowledge; and to knowledge, self-control; and to self-control, perseverance; and to perseverance, godliness; and to godliness, mutual affection; and to mutual affection, love.*

For if you possess these qualities in increasing measure, they will keep you from being ineffective and unproductive in your knowledge of our Lord Jesus Christ.

Make yourself available to the Holy Spirit, for He is Spirit and life! Resolve today to walk the paths of complete obedience. Throw open the gates of your mind to the Word of God. Open your ears and hear what the Spirit is saying today. Give your heavenly Father, Savior, and Holy Spirit the opportunity to speak to your listening ear.

A. T. Robertson explains in his Word Pictures of the New Testament that the words in Luke 24:45 translated as, "He opened He their mind" (*diênoixen autôn ton noun*) carries the same meaning as Paul's prayer for the spiritual eyes of the Ephesians to be opened.[86]

> *Then their eyes were opened and they recognized him, and he disappeared from their sight. They asked each other, "Were not our hearts burning within us while he talked with us on the road and opened the Scriptures to us?"*
>
> — Luke 24:31–32 (NIV)

> *I keep asking that the God of our Lord Jesus Christ, the glorious Father, may give you the Spirit of wisdom and revelation [understanding], so that you may know him [Jesus] better. I pray that the eyes of your heart may be enlightened in order that you may know the hope to which he has called you, the riches of his glorious*

inheritance in his holy people, and his incomparably
great power for us who believe.

— Ephesians 1:17–19 (NIV)

Robertson continues by saying,

Jesus had for many years been trying to open their
minds that they might understand the Scriptures about
the Him and now at last He makes one more effort in
the light of the Cross and the Resurrection. They can
now see better the will and way of God, but they will
still need the power of the Holy Spirit before they will
fully know the mind of Christ.[87]

Paul speaks of this same concept in Colossians 1:9 (NIV), which says,

For this reason, since the day we heard about you, we
have not stopped praying for you. We continually ask
God to fill you with the knowledge of his will through
all wisdom and understanding that the Spirit gives.

I encourage you to pray for the knowledge of his will through all spiritual wisdom and understanding. Ask Him to open your understanding so that you may know Him in the power of His resurrection and the fellowship of His sufferings. Pray He will reveal Himself to you and give you spiritual wisdom and understanding so you can minister fully and freely by His power and grace.

The Geneva Study Bible raises an important question:

If it surpasses the capacity of men, how can it be understood by any man, or how can you declare and preach it? By a special enlightening of God's Spirit, with which whoever is inspired, he can enter even into the very secrets of God.[88]

CHAPTER NINETEEN

Prophetic Understanding of Types and Shadows

They serve at a sanctuary that is a copy and shadow of what is in heaven. This is why Moses was warned when he was about to build the tabernacle: "See to it that you make everything according to the pattern shown you on the mountain."

— Hebrews 8:5 (NIV)

The law is only a shadow of the good things that are coming—not the realities themselves.

— Hebrews 10:1 (NIV)

Earlier in this book, I spoke of the spiritual light of God shining from the end of created or chronological time backward to the beginning and how the cross of Calvary casts a shadow by which we can understand the deeper things of God as we live the light of His Word. The Old Testament is filled with types, shadows, copies, pictures, and patterns of the things that were and still are to come. The Greek word for such things is *eikon*. An *eikon* is an image, figure, type, or likeness of the heavenly things. It speaks to the idea of something in the natural world used to reveal to us the image of the Son of God, into which true Christians are transformed.[89]

Biblical types are pictures or object lessons by which God taught His people concerning His grace and saving power. Through these biblical types and shadows, the Father in heaven was teaching His children (i.e., prior to the cross and resurrection of Jesus Christ) their "letters." Now on this side of the cross, our heavenly Father is teaching us through the prophetic ministry of the Holy Spirit to put the letters together. As the Holy Spirit arranges His words to us, they are arranged to spell Christ and nothing but Christ. In other words, every true type and shadow found in the Old Testament must be viewed as Christ-centric.[90]

If we begin at the "top" or "beginning" of the shadow of the cross, we will find ourselves in the book of Genesis. Genesis is the seed plot of the whole Bible. It is essential to the true understanding of its every part. And it is the foundation upon which all divine revelation rests and on which it is built. All streams of truth that originate in Genesis flow throughout the whole Bible and end in the book of Revelation.[91] Genesis is where we must begin in our understanding of all types, shadows, copies, pictures, and patterns.

In each of these categories, it might help if we viewed them as one sees an onion. First, an onion is a whole vegetable completely contained within an outer layer that can be seen, held, smelled, and tasted. Second, it has many layers to it. Third, the farther one slices into the heart of an onion, the deeper the aroma and the stronger the taste. Finally, each layer can be peeled off and examined only to reveal another layer to be tasted and examined. In all of the truths and revelations we have from the book of Genesis, there are many layers to each of them, and like an onion, each layer takes us deeper into God's understanding and wisdom.

An example is water. Water is the first part of the earth mentioned in the book of Genesis. Genesis 1:2 (NIV) (emphasis added by the author) says, "Now the earth was formless and empty, darkness was over the surface of the deep, *and the Spirit of God was hovering over the waters.*" The Spirit of God or Holy Spirit is connected, therefore, to the subject of water in the Scripture and is a type of the Holy Spirit. Naturally speaking, water is everywhere in our atmosphere, where it supplies the lungs, conveys sound, diffuses odors, drives ships, supports fire, gives rain, and so much more.[92] On the other hand, when speaking of water as being a type of the Holy Spirit (like water), He fills our atmosphere, provides life-giving nourishment to our breath, falls like rain on the thirsty soul, flows like a river from those who believe, washes and cleanses, provides life to everyone He touches, moves us along in the direction of God's will for our lives, and so much more. His ministry and work are inexhaustible.

The New Testament book of Hebrews reveals the use of prophetic words such as type, copy, shadow, and pattern. Each one reveals, in some degree or another, spiritual knowledge, as well as prophetic wisdom and understanding. This is because the general idea of each is the common revelation of "likeness." A person, event, or thing is shown to be fashioned or appointed to resemble another, especially in a futuristic sense; the one is made to answer to the other in some essential feature; in some particulars, the one matches the other. The two are called type and antitype, and the link which binds them together is the correspondence, the similarity, of the one with the other. Webster defines such as either a simile or metaphor.

A simile is a comparison of two things which, however different in other respects, have some strong point or points of resemblance; by which comparison, the character or qualities of a thing are illustrated or presented in an impressive light.[93]

While a metaphor is a short similitude. It is a similitude reduced to a single word; or a word expressing similitude without the signs of comparison. Thus "that man is a fox" is a metaphor, but "that man is like a fox" is a similitude or comparison. So when I say, "The soldiers fought like lions," I use a similitude. In a *metaphor*, the similitude is contained in the name; a man is a fox, means that a man is as crafty as a fox.[94]

Another word used in the New Testament is *shadow*. It is translated from the Greek word *skia*. Such is found in Hebrews 10:1 (KJV), "For the law having a shadow of good things to come," as if the substance or reality that was still future cast its shadow back into the old economy. "Shadow" implies dimness and transitoriness, but it also implies a measure of resemblance between the one and the other.[95] Another Greek word for shadow is *tupos*. *Tupos* means a copy or pattern. In the technical sense, a pattern shows in conformity to which a thing must be made, and in a doctrinal sense, it is a person or thing prefiguring a future (Messianic) person or thing.[96] An example of such includes Noah's ark, Abraham's altar on Moriah, the tabernacle of Moses, and Solomon's temple are a shadow of the promised Messiah of the Hebrew people.

When it comes to prophetic ministry, the types, shadows, and patterns of the Bible must possess three well-defined qualities. First, they must be a true picture of the person or the thing it represents or prefigures. An example is Aaron, as a high priest, is a rough figure of Christ, the great high priest. Second, the revealed type, shadow, or pattern must be of divine appointment. As centuries sometimes lie between the type and its accomplishment in the antitype, only the infinite wisdom of God alone can ordain the one to be the picture of the other. Third, such always prefigures something future. A scriptural type, shadow, or pattern always looks to the future; an element of prediction must necessarily be in it.[97] We see this in Hebrews 8:5, where the tabernacle is a shadow of the real that will be revealed to us in heaven.

The first example I want to mention is the typical prophetic view of the Feast of the Passover instituted by God in preparation for Moses leading the nation of Israel out of Egypt. For many years there has been no question as to the spiritual meaning of the Passover. Jesus Christ is our Passover. He has been sacrificed for us and as us, as the Passover Lamb was sacrificed for and as the firstborn son in every Hebrew household. And just as Jesus in our Passover Lamb, He, too, is our unleavened bread. Therefore, the apostle Paul exhorts the Corinthians to keep the Feast of Unleavened Bread, "not with the old leaven, neither with the leaven of malice and wickedness; but with the unleavened bread of sincerity and truth" (1 Corinthians 5:8, KJV).

In this passage, Paul reveals that the Word of God has a revelational aspect to it, and that aspect is present within any current interpretation if it is in agreement with the context and the interpretation of "as like" Scripture. In the words of Renee Bloch, Scripture "always concerns a living word addressed personally to the people of God and to each of its members." According to Miss Bloch, the essence of the midrashic procedure was a contemporization of Scripture in order to apply it to or make it meaningful for the current situation. It can be seen, then, in interpretive renderings of the Hebrew text.[98]

A scriptural example of this is found in Peter's sermon on the day of Pentecost,

> *But this is that which was spoken by the prophet Joel;*
> *And it shall come to pass in the last days, saith God,*
> *I will pour out of my Spirit upon all flesh: and your*
> *sons and your daughters shall prophesy, and your young*
> *men shall see visions, and your old men shall dream*
> *dreams: And on my servants and on my handmaidens I*
> *will pour out in those days of my Spirit; and they shall*
> *prophesy.*
>
> — Acts 2:16–18 (KJV)

The keywords are "this is that." These words speak to what "was" to the present truth being prophetically revealed to first the speaker and then to the hearers. The apostle Peter felt such was important as he then related such to the churches of Asia Minor when he wrote, "Wherefore I will not be negligent to put you always in remembrance of these things, though ye know them, and be established in the present truth" (2 Peter 1:12, KJV).

This type of spiritual prophetic understanding can be seen in the prophetic view of numbers, colors, names, etc., found in the book of beginnings, the book of Genesis. Let's look first at where our numbers originate. They originate with God *in the beginning*.

"And there was evening, and there was morning—the first day" (Genesis 1:5, NIV).

> *And the earth was without form, and void; and darkness was upon the face of the deep. And the Spirit of God moved upon the face of the waters.*
>
> — Genesis 1:2 (KJV)

- DAY 1: the number of God and beginnings. "In the beginning God" (Genesis 1:1, NIV). And, "Hear, O Israel: The LORD our God, the LORD is one" (Deuteronomy 6:4, NIV).
- DAY 2: the number of separations and agreements. "And God said, 'Let there be a vault between the waters to separate water from water'" (Genesis 1:6, NIV). And, "Do two walk together unless they have agreed to do so?" (Amos 3:3, NIV).
- DAY 3: the number of divine purpose and production. "Then God said, 'Let the land produce vegetation: seed-bearing plants and trees on the land that bear fruit with seed in it, according to their various kinds.' And it was so" (Genesis 1:11, NIV). And, "Therefore go and make disciples of all nations, baptizing them in the name of the Father and of the Son and of the Holy Spirit, and teaching them to obey everything I have commanded you" (Matthew 28:19–20, NIV).
- DAY 4: the number of created government. "God made two great lights—the greater light to govern the day and the lesser light to govern the night"

(Genesis 1:16, NIV). And, "He rules the world in righteousness and judges the peoples with justice" (Psalm 9:8, NIV).

- DAY 5: the number of life and grace. "And God said, 'Let the water teem with living creatures'" (Genesis 1:20, NIV). And, "The Spirit of God has made me; the breath of the Almighty gives me life" (Job 33:4, NIV).
- DAY 6: the number of mankind and work. "Then God said, 'Let us make mankind in our image, in our likeness'" (Genesis 1:26, NIV). And, "Six days you shall labor and do all your work" (Exodus 20:9, NIV).
- DAY 7: the number of fullness and Sabbath rest.

By the seventh day God had finished the work he had been doing; so on the seventh day he rested from all his work. Then God blessed the seventh day and made it holy, because on it he rested from all the work of creating that he had done.

— Genesis 2:2–3 (NIV)

Genesis is also where color was created. We know that there are over one million colors within the spectrum of color. But, in the seven colors of the rainbow, we can see great meaning, including the seven redemptive names of God represented in the Old Testament. Each one describes the seven redemptive aspects of His character, and the rainbow of color was first revealed in Genesis 9:13 (KJV) and completed in Revelation 4:3 (KJV),

*"I do set my bow in the cloud, and it shall be for a
token of a covenant between me and the earth."*

*"And he that sat was to look upon like a jasper and a
sardine stone: and there was a rainbow round about
the throne, in sight like unto an emerald."*

The seven colors of the rainbow are:

- *Red,* which as a type represents righteousness,
  the blood of the Lamb, and **Jehovah-Tsidkenu**.
  Jeremiah 23:6 (NIV) says, "In his days Judah will
  be saved and Israel will live in safety. This is the
  name by which he will be called: The LORD Our
  Righteousness."
- *Orange,* which is a type of victory, overcoming,
  and **Jehovah-Nissi**. Exodus 17:15 (NIV) says,
  "Moses built an altar and called it The LORD is
  my Banner."
- *Yellow* typifies God's Presence, the council of God,
  and **Jehovah-Shammah**. This Name signifies God's
  Presence which is not only with us but fills the
  whole earth. The prophet Ezekiel said, "And the
  name of the city from that time on will be: The
  LORD is there" (Ezekiel 48:35, NIV).
- *Green* is representative of peace, life, and mercy;
  Jehovah-Shalom. The Old Testament uses the
  word *"peace"* in very practical ways, especially for
  the well-being of our lives. "Gideon built an altar

to the LORD there and called it The LORD Is Peace" (Judges 6:24, NIV).

- *Blue*, God's healing power, wholeness, soundness, **Jehovah-Rapha**. He said,

If you listen carefully to the LORD your God and do what is right in his eyes, if you pay attention to his commands and keep all his decrees, I will not bring on you any of the diseases I brought on the Egyptians, for I am the LORD, who heals you.

— Exodus 15:26 (NIV)

- *Indigo* is a type of the Lord leading His sheep. Shepherd: **Jehovah-Ra-ah**. Isaiah 40:11 (NIV) says, "He tends his flock like a shepherd: He gathers the lambs in his arms and carries them close to his heart; he gently leads those that have young." And Psalm 23:1 (NIV) says, "The LORD is my shepherd, I lack nothing." The Lord Jesus is the good shepherd, great shepherd, and chief shepherd (John 10:11; Hebrews 13:20; 1 Peter 5:4).
- *Violet* represents wealth and provision: **Jehovah-Jireh**. Genesis 22:13–14 (NIV) says,

Abraham looked up and there in a thicket he saw a ram caught by its horns. He went over and took the ram and sacrificed it as a burnt offering instead of his son. So Abraham called that place The LORD Will Provide. And to this day it is said, "On the mountain of the LORD it will be provided."

Types are also found in some aspects of the clothing worn or used in the Old Testament. Examples include Aaron's priestly garments, the clothing of Jonathan (Saul's son), and the clothes, both worn and torn, by Elisha in 2 Kings 2. A great example of such is the mantle of Elijah. Elijah's mantle was a physical sign of the anointing of the Holy Spirit that "rested" upon him. He cast his mantle upon Elisha (his protégé) in 1 Kings 19:19. Elisha then asked Elijah for a "double portion of your spirit" in 2 Kings 2:9 (NIV). Elijah said that such would be given to him if he saw Elijah leave.

Not long after Elijah spoke, a chariot of fire and horses came between the two, separating them and picking Elijah up, taking him into heaven. The Scripture says the moment Elijah went up, his mantle came down. As Elijah (the person) ascended, the prophet's mantle (representing his anointing) fell from his shoulders and stayed on the earth to rest upon Elisha. Dr. Kelley Varner said, the parallel is obvious: Jesus ascended into heaven, but on the Day of Pentecost His Spirit came down. Yes, Jesus ascended, but the anointing (*christos*) of the Anointed One, remained in the earth to rest upon His Church.

To cite my friend and colleague Dr. Kelley Varner again, in his message at the church I pastored many years ago in Tulsa, Oklahoma, Dr. Varner shared that the Hebrew word for "mantle" in the 2 Kings passage is the feminine form of the Hebrew word *'addiyrr*, which means "something ample; wide, large; figuratively, and powerful." It is translated in many different ways, such as "excellent, famous, gallant, glorious, goodly, lordly, mighty, noble, principal, and worthy" in the King James Version of the Bible. This "double portion of the anointing" literally means "the portion of the firstborn," and it belongs to all of us and to each one of us, who are heirs of God and joint heirs with Jesus Christ! (see Romans 8).

Both Varner's and Warnock's understanding presented here would be regarded as charismatic exegesis, which was one of the things used by Jesus (during His ministry on Earth and the work of inspired persons such as Daniel, Ezekiel, and the apostles Paul and Peter). And remember, all typology, including New Testament typology, is and must be thoroughly Christological in its focus. Jesus is the "prophet like Moses" (Acts 3:22) who, in His passion, brings the old covenant to its proper goal and end (Romans 10:4; Hebrews 10:9) and establishes a new covenant (Luke 22:20, 29). As the messianic "son of David," i.e., "Son of God," He is the recipient of the promises and ascriptions given to the Davidic kings.[99]

All typology, including New Testament typology, is and must be thoroughly Christological in its focus.

Leonard Goppelt has set forth the definitive marks of typological interpretation. He said they were,

> *(1) Unlike allegory, typological exegesis regards the words of Scripture not as metaphors hiding a deeper meaning but as the record of historical events out of whose literal sense the meaning of the text arises. (2) Unlike the "history of religions" exegesis, it seeks the meaning of current, New Testament situations from a particular history, the salvation-history of Israel. (3) Like rabbinic midrash, typological exegesis interprets the text in terms of contemporary situations, but it does so with historical distinctions that are lacking in*

rabbinic interpretation (4) It identifies a typology in terms of two basic characteristics, historical correspondence, and escalation, in which the divinely ordered prefigurement finds a complement in the subsequent and greater event).[99]

— Page 244

All this speaks to several things that all prophetic people must consider. First, all prophetic ministry, including the interpretation of types and shadows, must begin with and end in Christ Jesus. Second, all Scripture must be correctly interpreted by the Scripture itself. Scripture cannot be interpreted by personal "eisegesis," including by one's historical or modern theology. Scripture must be compared with Scripture. Then the definition of the Hebrew, Aramaic, Greek, and English words must be compared and examined in context along with their use in other Scripture. Third, historical, theological, and prophetic writers must then be considered, such as E. Earle Ellis, E. W. Bullinger, George Warnock, and Kelley Varner. And finally, where is the modern church? What is happening? What is God saying to this generation? Nation? People? Church? Or person? This includes the insights provided by George Barna and others, as well as the teachings of current national or international prophetic teachers.

I know this may sound like a lot of work. But, without it, we can become like the Pharisees Jesus addressed in Matthew 22:29 (NIV), "Jesus replied, 'You are in error because you do not know the Scriptures or the power of God.'" On the road to Emmaus, Jesus exhorted two disciples beginning with Moses and all the prophets. He explained to them what was said in all the Scriptures concerning Himself (see Luke 24:27). Then Paul wrote to his young pastor Timothy in 2 Timothy 3:14–17 (NIV),

> *But as for you, continue in what you have learned and have become convinced of, because you know those from whom you learned it, and how from infancy you have known the Holy Scriptures, which are able to make you wise for salvation through faith in Christ Jesus. All Scripture is God-breathed and is useful for teaching, rebuking, correcting and training in righteousness, so that the servant of God may be thoroughly equipped for every good work.*

Let us also pray the Spirit of wisdom and understanding will bring understanding and insight to all to study, learn, say, and write.

CONCLUSION:

Prophetic Insights

*Seek the Lord while he may be found; call on him
while he is near.*

— Isaiah 55:6 (NIV)

We find ourselves in a very difficult place. We are participants in a complex situation. The spiritual movement that began at the turn of the twentieth century is beginning to fade, and the new one is just barely coming into view. As members of the present move of God, we continue to experience the blessings given to our parents and grandparents. Many of us can testify to experiencing the great goodness of God as a child, an adult, and now as senior adults. But we are also experiencing the limitations of the present moment. It reminds me of the period the first apostles experienced between the resurrection and the Day of Pentecost.

For His apostles, the events of the week prior to the cross were difficult at best. Then the crucifixion brutalized their faith and practically destroyed their hope. Three days later, they experienced untold joy! They saw Jesus was alive, not as a ghost or apparition, but in resurrected flesh. I have no doubt most of them thought that the life they experienced just following the resurrection was going to be the end of the story. But God had other plans. Jesus had told them that He wanted them to go to all the world, telling everyone what they had seen and learned. He also said He would be with them until the end of the age (Matthew 28:18–20).

I'm sure, in their mind, they probably thought He was staying with them in His physically resurrected form for the rest of their lives. I doubt they understood that He was leaving, so they could experience a greater dimension of glory. Why else would they have asked Him, "Lord, are you at this time going to restore the kingdom to Israel?" (Acts 1:6, NIV). Instead of giving them what they expected,

> *He said to them: "It is not for you to know the times or dates the Father has set by his own authority. But you will receive power when the Holy Spirit comes on you; and you will be my witnesses in Jerusalem, and in all Judea and Samaria, and to the ends of the earth."*
>
> — Acts 1:7–8 (NIV)

It was then Jesus "was taken up before their very eyes, and a cloud hid him from their sight" (verse 9, NIV).

Put yourself in their shoes. At that moment, they really did not want Him to leave. They still did not understand. Why else would they stand staring, "looking intently up into the sky as He was going"? Then,

> *Suddenly two men dressed in white stood beside them. "Men of Galilee," they said, "why do you stand here looking into the sky? This same Jesus, who has been*

taken from you into heaven, will come back in the
same way you have seen him go into heaven."

— Acts 1:10–11 (NIV)

Only then did they return to Jerusalem. Many believe that the Lord's time of ascension coincides with the time spoken of by Paul in 1 Corinthians 15:6, when Jesus appeared to five hundred of the brothers. If that be the case, only one-hundred-and-twenty made it all the way until the spiritual and prophetic experience that happened on the Day of Pentecost.

When the day of Pentecost came, they were all together
in one place. Suddenly a sound like the blowing of a
violent wind came from heaven and filled the whole
house where they were sitting. They saw what seemed
to be tongues of fire that separated and came to rest
on each of them. All of them were filled with the Holy
Spirit and began to speak in other tongues as the Spirit
enabled them.

— Acts 2:1–4 (NIV)

Like those first apostles, there is a remnant of believers who are enjoying the benefits of God's heavenly treasures and, at the same time, are being given insight concerning the pattern which has been revealed to us. And that pattern? That both the previous spiritual movements, revivals, etc. (previously called a reformation, revival, or awakening) and future ones that will take place will come and go in a cyclical fashion.

Solomon said, "What has been will be again, what has been done will be done again; there is nothing new under the sun" (Ecclesiastes 1:9, NIV). With each new revolution, there is a going out and a coming in, a coming in and a going out. Such was the case with Abraham and Isaac, Moses and Joshua, and even Jesus and His disciples. Such reveals the kingdom of God's formation and shape (on the earth). With each revolution, Christ is directing and leading His church toward the dawning of a new age when His kingdom is revealed from heaven in all His glory.

Let us then ask, what will be the Lord's purpose in this coming season? It is actually very simple. The church is being invited by the Holy Spirit to overcome the current difficulties of life so that we might learn to be and become the people He has called us to be. He is using His knowledge, understanding, wisdom, grace, and more so that we might be molded into the image of Christ and become a holy people who think, act, and speak like Christ Jesus. In doing so, we are to show forth the praises of Him, who has called us out of darkness and into His marvelous light (1 Peter 2:9).

There is a clarion call beginning to take place for those chosen and blessed in Him, by Him, and for Him to be His corporate body on Earth.

Believers are to be one in Him and with each other. The Scripture calls us *sons of God* (Hebrews 2:9), *a chosen generation* (1 Peter 2:9), *Abraham's seed* (Galatians 3:29), *Zion* (Hebrews 12:22), *His temple* (1 Corinthians 6:19), *living stones* (1 Peter 2:5), and many other titles and references. For we are a many-membered body, and Christ is the head.

Give glory and honor, power, and praise unto our master and Lord! There is no one above Him. He has been exalted to the place above all principality and power and might, and dominion, and every name that is named both in this world and the world to come. His Name is above every name (Philippians 2:9–11).

Prepare yourself. The future will look nothing like the past. Fresh knowledge, understanding, and wisdom of the glorious treasures found in Christ are coming toward us. As chronological time moves forward (*chronos*), we will be coming into a new season (*kairos*). It will be a time when greater dimensions of spiritual things are brought to light. Many folks will see it as a season of great crisis, while others will view it as a new opportunity to experience the treasures of heaven.

These "periods and points" of time shall be distinguished by awesome manifestations of spiritual gifts, including signs, wonders, and miracles. There will be fresh revelation concerning the kingdom of God on Earth. The revelation will grow deeper and wider by including more people and revealing fresh spiritual understanding and wisdom as well as the manifestation of prophetic gifts. Already deep is calling out to deep (Psalm 42:7). The Spirit is searching the hearts of men to reveal the deep things of God to those who will hear it (1 Corinthians 2:10). As Daniel said (2:20–22, NIV),

> *Praise be to the name of God for ever and ever; wisdom and power are his. He changes times and seasons; he deposes kings and raises up others. He gives wisdom to the wise and knowledge to the discerning. He reveals deep and hidden things; he knows what lies in darkness, and light dwells with him.*

In the Old Testament, Moses, Elijah, Elisha, Daniel, David, Solomon, and Isaiah were given great spiritual knowledge, understanding, and wisdom. But none compared to Jesus. God Himself, living on the earth (Immanuel), revealed more spiritual insight and revelation than anyone before Him. And since His resurrection from the dead and the subsequent outpouring of the Holy Spirit, there have been both great men and women to whom were given tremendous illumination concerning the treasures of heaven. Apostles like Paul, John, and Peter, as well as several of the early church fathers (like Clement of Rome and Ignatius), received spectacular revelational knowledge concerning Jesus Christ, the kingdom of God, the ministry of the Holy Spirit, and much, much more.

Since then, there have been individuals like Martin Luther, John Calvin, Isaac Newton, John Wesley, E. W. Bullinger, Charles H. Spurgeon, A. W. Tozer, Fanny Crosby, Amy Carmichael, Jonathan Edwards, Aimee Semple McPherson, James Hudson Taylor, Dwight Moody, and my friend and colleague Kelley Varner, just to name a few. These people and many, many more throughout the chapters of "His-story" were given spiritual insight, understanding, and wisdom. They have been and continue to be an encouragement and inspiration to millions of people around the world through their books and writings.

When the trials of life are about to get us down, or the pressures of the world seem almost overwhelming, remember there have been those who have gone before you. In many instances, they faced great difficulty, even to the point of death. They continued steadfastly in the faith and became known as people of great honor, faith, strength, and purpose. In other words, like the team that found the buried treasure of the Maravillas, these and others made room in their heart for new knowledge, understanding, and wisdom. They experienced firsthand the transforming power of God. Each was given a great amount of grace that enabled them to bring salt and light to the time and season they lived in. In doing so, they influenced many future generations for Christ.

The writings of several of the people I have mentioned have stood out to me. The Lord used both men and women to spur me on toward a greater pursuit of Christ Jesus. I have mentioned one of them, Dr. Charles S. Price, several times in this book. I was in college when I first learned of Dr. Price and his ministry. I learned he was the pastor of a very liberal congregational church in Lodi, California. In 1921, he attended a service being held by the evangelist Aimee Semple McPherson and did so for the purpose of exposing her as a fraud. He was convinced that the so-called "conversions and miracles" that were being testified about could be explained as metaphysical or psychological. He fully expected McPherson's services to be rife with wild fanaticism. After listening to the powerful message that fateful night (which he said later was both biblical and compelling), Dr. Price experienced and was overwhelmed by God's wonderous and marvelous grace. Instead of being focused on exposing what he had previously believed to be biblically wrong and misguided, he found himself responding to McPherson's altar call. That night he dedicated His life to Christ and was literally overwhelmed by the power of the Holy Spirit.

Dr. Price went back to Lodi and shared his experience with his congregation. The move of God (we now call the Pentecostal movement) filled his life and ministry. Soon his church became the epicenter of a revival that swept all of central and northern

California. Then, the shift sent ripples into Oregon, Washington, Idaho, and Western Canada. Dr. Price left the pastorate and began traveling throughout the western part of the United States and Canada, telling his story and sharing the fresh knowledge, understanding, and spiritual wisdom God was pouring into him. There were hundreds and even thousands of documented healings and miracles.

According to one biography written about him and posted online by the Healing and Revival Press (visit www.healingandrevival.com), the ministry of Charles S. Price touched people as had not been seen since the Great Awakening. In 1923, Price preached to over 250,000 people in a three-week period, and many were healed. Everywhere he went, he saw miraculous healings in his meetings, and thousands came to Christ. His organization counted over 35,000 conversions in 1928 alone.

While many ministries shut down or were severely curtailed during the 1930s due to the Great Depression, the ministry of Charles S. Price continued to draw thousands to his meetings. In the late 1930s, he ministered in Norway, England, Egypt, Palestine, Turkey, Syria, Lebanon, and Italy, as well as continuing to speak throughout the northern part of the United States. In 1939, Price estimated that he had traveled over a million miles on evangelistic campaigns since he began in 1922. His schedule was demanding. At meetings where he was the main speaker, he would speak two or three times a day and often pray for people to be healed well into the night.[100]

In my life, God used Dr. Price's book, *The Real Faith*, to inspire me toward greater depths and higher heights in Him. I received new insight and a greater awareness of the available treasures of heaven from almost every page. My new inspiration did not come and go. Nor did it end with reading that one book. With each page, I was encouraged by the Holy Spirit to go on my own hunt for more of heaven's treasure, and with every passing week. I found myself praying more often, worshipping with more passion, and studying the Word of God with much more focus and intent. At the time, I did not understand how important or glorious the treasure would become to me. But through His understanding, the Holy Spirit taught me many of the truths shared in this book and others I have written previously about. Soon, a new hunger and appreciation for heaven's treasures and values took shape within my heart and life.

Since that time, I have continued to hunt for spiritual treasure. After fifty years of ministry, I still have an insatiable hunger and thirst for more of the things of God. For over forty years, I have held to and experienced the reward of this promise from the Sermon on the Mount, "Blessed are those who hunger and thirst for righteousness, for they will be filled" (Matthew 5:6, NIV).

I am convinced that the coming prophetic ministry explosion that I see on the horizon will change the lives of millions and billions of people (this includes your life as well). Our Lord wants you to live a life filled with His power and presence. I encourage you to seek to encounter, embrace, and enjoy all that God has for your life. And, once He begins filling your life to the brim and running it over, I exhort you to give that which you are being given to others. As you freely receive, freely give. For as you give, God will give even more. Jesus said one day to His disciples, "The knowledge of the secrets of the kingdom of heaven has been given to you, but not to them. Whoever has will be given more, and they will have an abundance" (Matthew 13:11–12, NIV).

See yourself as God sees you, as His personal treasure chest! You have become His place of safekeeping, where He is storing the treasures of heaven. If you continue to open your heart and offer yourself to Him, He will continue to fill your life with the glorious treasures of His goodness and grace. He also will withhold no good thing from you (Psalm 84:11), so I encourage you to go hunting for treasure today and get ready for the night is almost over; morning is about to break over the spiritual horizon!

For where your treasure is, there your heart will be also.

— Matthew 6:21 (NIV)

ABOUT THE AUTHOR

Robert Stone has been in his Lord's ministry for over fifty years. He and his wife, Susan, have been involved in full-time ministry since 1977. Known to many as a missionary, teacher, mentor, and spiritual father, Robert sees his personal mission as to help people become who and what God purposed them to be from the beginning. His results-driven approach has stimulated many to become all they can be for the cause of Christ.

Robert continues to write, travel, and teach. His articles, books, and Bible study materials will continue to bless others long after his lifetime. He has traveled to over twenty countries and forty states. His achievements include the development and construction of churches and Bible schools in the United States, Mexico, Jamaica, Haiti, Curacao, Honduras, Costa Rica, Bolivia, Uganda, Kenya, Tanzania, and Malawi. He is the author of several books on leadership, prayer, and personal growth. His best-selling books, *Gifts of the Ascended Christ* and *The Altar of His Presence*, have touched people around the world.

Robert's prayer for you is that you enter, embrace, and enjoy a wonderful and exciting relationship with the Lord Jesus Christ by and through the ministry of the Holy Spirit. He prays that you will be moved from faith to faith, from strength to strength, and from glory to glory.

Robert has been married to the love of his life, Susan, for over forty-seven years. Together they have three children—Talitha, Tanyka, and Tyler.

END NOTES

1   Thayer and Smith. "Greek Lexicon entry *Metatithemi*." "The NAS New Testament Greek Lexicon." 1999.

2   January 2020 State of the Church Report, George Barna, *Barna Research Group*, January 2020.

3   Stabile, Angelica. "Sunken Jewels, Buried Treasure Uncovered in the Bahamas from Iconic 17th Century Spanish Shipwreck." Fox News, August 6, 2022. https://www.foxnews.com/lifestyle/sunken-jewels-buried-trea-sures-uncovered-bahamas-17th-century-spanish-shipwreck.

4   Ibid.

5   *Webster's 1828 American Dictionary of the English Language*, s.v. "Value."

6   Ibid.

7   "Intrinsic vs. Extrinsic Value." The Stanford Encyclopedia of Philosophy. Copyright by The Metaphysics Research Lab, Department of Philosophy, Stanford University. Library of Congress Catalog Data: ISSN 1095–505.

8   James Orr, Ed., *International Standard Bible Encyclopedia*, s.v. "Treasure," http://studylight.org/encyclopedias/isb/view.cgi?number=8829.

9   Strong, *Strong's Exhaustive Concordance*, G4301, H2344.

10 Andrew R. Fausset, *Fausset's Bible Dictionary*, s.v. "Heaven," http://www.studylight.org/dictionaries/fbd/view. cgi?n=1560.

11 Easton, Matthew George, Ed. *Easton's Bible Dictionary*. 3rd ed. N. p., 1897. http://kingjamesbibledictionary.com/ Dictionary/heaven.

12 Andrew R. Fausset, *Fausset's Bible Dictionary*, s.v. "Heaven," http://www.studylight.org/dictionaries/fbd/view.cgi?n=1560

13 Ibid.

14 Ibid.

15 https://scied.ucar.edu/learning-zone/atmosphere/what-is-at-mosphere. Copyright UCAR 2023. P.O. Box 3000, Boulder, CO 80307-3000. This material is based upon work supported by the National Center for Atmospheric Research, a major facility sponsored by the National Science Foundation and managed by the University Corporation for Atmospheric Research.

16 James Orr, Ed., *International Standard Bible Encyclopedia*, s.v. "God, Names of," http://studylight.org/encyclopedias/ isb/view.cgi?number=3836.

17 Alcorn, Randy. *Heaven: A Comprehensive Guide to Everything the Bible Says About Our Eternal Home*. Tyndale Momentum. Hardcover edition. October 1, 2004.

18 James Orr, Ed., *International Standard Bible Encyclopedia*, s.v. "Anthropology," https://studylight.org/encyclopedias/ eng/isb/a/anthropology.html.

19 James Orr, Ed., *International Standard Bible Encyclopedia*, s.v. "Sin 1," http://studylight.org/encyclopedias/isb/view.cgi?number=8120.

20 *Webster's 1828 American Dictionary of the English Language*, s.v. "Idol."

21 Strong, *Strong's Exhaustive Concordance*, H1586.

22 James Orr, Ed., *International Standard Bible Encyclopedia*, s.v. "Logos," http://studylight.org/encyclopedias/isb/view.cgi?number=5529.

23 Strong, *Strong's Exhaustive Concordance*, H5051. Finisher.

24 Robertson, "Commentary on Hebrews 12:2," *Robertson's Word Pictures of the New Testament*. http://biblestudytools.com/commentaries/robertsons-word-pictures/hebrews/hebrews-12–2.html.

25 Ephesians 1:3 – Maclaren's Expositions of Holy Scripture – Bible Commentaries – StudyLight.org. https://www.studylight.org/commentaries/eng/mac/ephesians-1.html.

26 "Déjà Vu." Wikipedia, n.d. https://en.wikipedia.org/wiki/D%C3%A9j%C3%A0_vu.

27 James Orr, Ed., *International Standard Bible Encyclopedia*, s.v. "Glory," http://studylight.org/encyclopedias/isb/view.cgi?number=3891.

28 "Shekinah." The Lockman Foundation, PO Box 2279, La Habra, CA 90631, Study Light 2001-2023. https://www.studylight.org/dictionaries/eng/web/s/shekinah.html.

29 James Orr, Ed., *International Standard Bible Encyclopedia*, s.v. "Bless," http://studylight.org/encyclopedias/isb/view.cgi?number=1546.

30 Ibid.

31 Ibid.

32 James Orr, Ed., *International Standard Bible Encyclopedia*, s.v. "Love," http://studylight.org/encyclopedias/isb/view.cgi?number=5355.

33 James Orr, Ed., *International Standard Bible Encyclopedia*, s.v. "Heart," http://studylight.org/encyclopedias/isb/view.cgi?number=4184.

34 James Orr, Ed., *International Standard Bible Encyclopedia*, s.v. "Love," http://studylight.org/encyclopedias/isb/view.cgi?number=5355

35 Romans 5:5 – Maclaren's Expositions of Holy Scripture – Bible Commentaries – StudyLight.org. https://www.studylight.org/commentaries/eng/mac/romans-5-5.html.

36 Strong, *Strong's Exhaustive Concordance*, H993.

37 James Orr, Ed., *International Standard Bible Encyclopedia*, s.v. "John, the Apostle," http://studylight.org/encyclopedias/isb/view.cgi?number=5060.

38 Strong, *Strong's Exhaustive Concordance*, H1097.

39 Dr. Patrick Oben. https://patrickoben.com/spiritual-metamorphosis-trigger/. Copyright Patrick Oben Ministries, Inc. PO Box 379, Ankeny, IA 50021–2022.

40 Robertson, "Commentary on 2 Corinthians 4:7," *Robertson's Word Pictures of the New Testament*. http://biblestudytools.com/commentaries/robertsons-word-pictures/2 Corinthians/2 Corinthians-4-7.html.

41 *Webster's 1828 American Dictionary of the English Language,* s.v. "Precept, Concept."

42 Lucado, Max. *An Act of Gratitude.* From The Secrets to the Good Life, Upwords Blog, Copyright 2023 Max Lucado.

43 P., Gene. "Benefits of Gratitude: 31 Powerful Reasons to Be More Grateful." Happier Human, n.d. https://www.happierhuman.com/benefits-of-gratitude/.

44 Strong, *Strong's Exhaustive Concordance,* H1097.

45 Strong, *Strong's Exhaustive Concordance,* H3408, H2817.

46 Strong, *Strong's Exhaustive Concordance,* H4102.

47 *Free Lexham Bible Dictionary.*

48 Renner, Rick. "The Humility of Christ." Renner Ministries, n.d. https://renner.org/article/the-humility-of-christ/.

49 James Orr, Ed., *International Standard Bible Encyclopedia,* s.v. "John, the Apostle," http://studylight.org/encyclopedias/isb/view.cgi?number=5060.

50 Ibid.

51 Ibid.

52 James Orr, Ed., *International Standard Bible Encyclopedia,* s.v. "Confidence," http://studylight.org/encyclopedias/isb/view.cgi?number=2255.

53 *Webster's 1828 American Dictionary of the English Language,* s.v. "Honor."

54 Strong, *Strong's Exhaustive Concordance,* G03515, H5091.

55 Robertson, "Commentary on John 5:22–23," *Robertson's Word Pictures of the New Testament.* http://biblestudytools.

com/commentaries/robertsons-word-pictures/John/John-5-22.htmal.

56 Barnes, Albert. "Commentary on Romans 12." "Barnes' Notes on the Whole Bible." https://www.studylight.org/ commentaries/eng/bnb/romans-12.html. 1870.

57 Ibid.

58 Strong, *Strong's Exhaustive Concordance*, H5293.

59 MLA. Spence-Jones, H. D. M., 1836–1917, editor. *The Pulpit Commentary*, Ephesians 5:21.

60 Andrew R. Fausset, *Fausset's Bible Dictionary*, s.v. "Prophet," http://www.studylight.org/dictionaries/fbd/view. cgi?n=2891.

61 "Isaiah 6 - Maclaren's Expositions of Holy Scripture - Bible Commentaries." StudyLight.org, n.d. https://www.study-light.org/commentaries/eng/mac/isaiah-6.html.

62 James Orr, Ed., *International Standard Bible Encyclopedia*, s.v. "Gnosticism," http://studylight.org/encyclopedias/isb/ view.cgi?number=3824.

63 Ibid.

64 Robertson, "Commentary on Colossians 2:2," *Robertson's Word Pictures Of the New Testament*. http://biblestudytools. com/commentaries/robertsons-word-pictures/Colossians/ Colossians-2-2.html.

65 Ibid.

66 Strong, *Strong's Exhaustive Concordance*, G4886, H4886.

67 Andrew R. Fausset, Fausset's Bible Dictionary, s.v. "Anoint," http://www.studylight.org/dictionaries/fbd/view.cgi?n=264.

68 Andrew R. Fausset, *Fausset's Bible Dictionary*, s.v. "Anoint," http://www.studylight.org/dictionaries/fbd/view.cgi?n=264.

69 Andrew R. Fausset, *Fausset's Bible Dictionary*, s.v. "Joshua," http://www.studylight.org/dictionaries/fbd/view. cgi?n=2041.

70 Ellis, E. Earle. "Introduction." Introduction. In *Prophecy and Hermeneutic in Early Christianity: New Testament Essays*, 13. Grand Rapids, MI: W.B. Eerdmans Pub. Co., 1980.

71 Horgan, Maurya P. *Pesharim: Qumran Interpretation Of Biblical Books*. Washington: Catholic Biblical Association of America, 1979.

72 Brooke, George J. "Prophetic Interpretation." In *Exegesis at Qumran: 4QFlorilegium in Its Jewish Context*, 244. Atlanta: Society of Biblical Literature, 2006.

73 Ellis, E. Earle. *Prophecy and Hermeneutic in Early Christianity: New Testament Essays*. Grand Rapids, MI: W.B. Eerdmans Pub. Co., 1980.

74 Ellis, E. Earle. *Prophecy and Hermeneutic in Early Christianity: New Testament Essays*. Copyright 1978 by J.C.B. Mohr (Paul Siebeck). Essay, *The Pneumatics and the Early Christian Mission* page 34.

75 Strong, *Strong's Exhaustive Concordance*, H1390.

76 Strong, *Strong's Exhaustive Concordance*, H1391.

77 Strong, *Strong's Exhaustive Concordance*, H5486.

78 Strong, *Strong's Exhaustive Concordance*, H5486.

79 "Romans 12 - Maclaren's Expositions of Holy Scripture - Bible Commentaries." StudyLight.org, n.d. https://www.studylight.org/commentaries/eng/mac/romans-12.html.

80 Ibid.

81 Strong, *Strong's Exhaustive Concordance*, H1243, H4152.

82 Strong, *Strong's Exhaustive Concordance*, H3056, H1108.

83 Strong, *Strong's Exhaustive Concordance*, H3056, 4578.

84 Strong, *Strong's Exhaustive Concordance*, H2386.

85 Ibid.

86 Robertson, "Commentary on Luke 24:45" *Robertson's Word Pictures of the New Testament.* http://biblestudytools.com/commentaries/robertsons-word-pictures/Luke/Luke-24-45.html.

87 Ibid.

88 Marsh, E. C. *Geneva Study Bible Notes.* 1587.

89 Strong, *Strong's Exhaustive Concordance*, G6754, H1504.

90 James Orr, Ed., *International Standard Bible Encyclopedia*, s.v. "Type," http://studylight.org/encyclopedias/isb/view.cgi?number=8887.

91 Strong, *Strong's Exhaustive Concordance*, G6754, H1504.

92 James Orr, Ed., *International Standard Bible Encyclopedia*, s.v. "Type," http://studylight.org/encyclopedias/isb/view.cgi?number=8887.

93 *Webster's 1828 American Dictionary of the English Language*, s.v. "Simile."

94 *Webster's 1828 American Dictionary of the English Language,* s.v. "Metaphor."

95 James Orr, Ed., *International Standard Bible Encyclopedia,* s.v. "Type," http://studylight.org/encyclopedias/isb/view. cgi?number=8887.

96 Strong, *Strong's Exhaustive Concordance,* G6754, H1504.

97 James Orr, Ed., International Standard Bible Encyclopedia, s.v. "Type," http://studylight.org/encyclopedias/isb/view. cgi?number=8887.

98 Gundry, Matthew, p. 125n. 9. R. Bloch, "Midrash," Dictionnaire de la Bible: Supplement (Paris) 5 (1957), 1266. Cf. B. B. Warfield, The Inspiration and Authority of the Bible (Philadelphia 1948), p. 148: "Scripture is thought of as the living voice of God speaking in all its parts directly to the reader;" M. Barth, "The Old Testament in Hebrews," Current Issues in New Testament Interpretation, ed. W. Klassen (New York 1962), pp. 58ff. Also see op. cit., 201 NEW TESTAMENT INTERPRETATION note 9 M. Hengel, The Son of God (London 1976), pp. 42–5.

99 Goppelt, Leonhard. *Typos: The typological interpretation of the old testament in the new.* Wipf & Stock, n.d.

100   Ibid.